U.S. Department
of Transportation

**Federal Aviation
Administration**

COMMERCIAL PILOT

Practical Test Standards

for

ROTORCRAFT

• *HELICOPTER*

August 2006

**FLIGHT STANDARDS SERVICE
Washington, DC 20591**

NOTE

Material in FAA-S-8081-16A will be effective August 1, 2006. All previous editions of the Commercial Pilot — Rotorcraft (Helicopter) Practical Test Standards will be obsolete as of this date.

FOREWORD

The Commercial Pilot—Rotorcraft (Helicopter) Practical Test Standards (PTS) book has been published by the Federal Aviation Administration (FAA) to establish the standards for commercial pilot certification practical tests for the rotorcraft category, helicopter classes. FAA inspectors and designated pilot examiners shall conduct practical tests in compliance with these standards. Flight instructors and applicants should find these standards helpful during training and when preparing for the practical test.

Joseph K. Tintera, Manager
Regulatory Support Division
Flight Standards Service

CONTENTS

SECTION 1: COMMERCIAL PILOT ROTORCRAFT—HELICOPTER

AREAS OF OPERATION:

APPENDIX 1

INTRODUCTION

General Information

The Flight Standards Service of the Federal Aviation Administration (FAA) has developed this practical test standard (PTS) to be used by examiners[1] when conducting commercial pilot—rotorcraft practical tests. Instructors are expected to use this PTS when preparing applicants for practical tests. Applicants should be familiar with this PTS and refer to these standards during their training.

The FAA gratefully acknowledges the valuable assistance provided by many individuals, companies, and organizations throughout the aviation community who have contributed their time and talent in assisting with the revision of this practical test standard.

This PTS may be purchased from the Superintendent of Documents, U.S. Government Printing Office (GPO), Washington, DC 20402-9325, or from GPO's web site.

http://bookstore.gpo.gov

This PTS is also available for download, in pdf format, from the Regulatory Support Division's (AFS-600) web site.

http://www.faa.gov/about/office_org/headquarters_offices/avs/offices/afs/afs600

This PTS is published by the U.S. Department of Transportation, Federal Aviation Administration, Airman Testing Standards Branch, AFS-630, P.O. Box 25082, Oklahoma City, OK 73125.

Comments regarding this handbook should be sent, in e-mail form, to the following address.

AFS630comments@faa.gov

---

[1] The word "examiner" denotes either the FAA Inspector, FAA designated pilot examiner, or other authorized person who conducts the practical test.

FAA-S-8081-16A

Practical Test Standard Concept

Title 14 of the Code of Federal Regulations (14 CFR) part 61 species the areas in which knowledge and skill must be demonstrated by the applicant before the issuance of a commercial pilot certificate or rating. The CFRs provide the flexibility that permits the FAA to publish practical test standards containing the AREAS OF OPERATION and specific TASKs in which competency must be demonstrated. The FAA will revise this PTS whenever it is determined that changes are needed in the interest of safety. *Adherence to the provisions of the regulations and the practical test standards is mandatory for the evaluation of commercial pilot applicants.*

Practical Test Book Description

This test book contains the following Commercial Pilot Practical Test Standards:

> **Section 1**   Rotorcraft—Helicopter

The Commercial Pilot—Rotorcraft Practical Test Standards include the AREAS OF OPERATION and TASKs for the issuance of an initial commercial pilot certificate and for the addition of category and/or class ratings to that certificate.

AREAS OF OPERATION are phases of the practical test arranged in a logical sequence within this standard. They begin with Preflight Preparation and end with Post-flight Procedures. The examiner may conduct the practical test in any sequence that will result in a complete and efficient test. *However, the ground portion of the practical test must be accomplished before the flight portion.*

TASKs are titles of knowledge areas, flight procedures, or maneuvers appropriate to an AREA OF OPERATION.

REFERENCE identifies the publication(s) that describe(s) the TASK. Descriptions of TASKs are not included in the standards because this information can be found in the current issue of the listed reference. Publications other than those listed may be used, for references if their content conveys substantially the same meaning as the referenced publications.

NOTE is used to emphasize special considerations required in the AREA OF OPERATION or TASK.

These practical test standards are based on the following reference list:

14 CFR part 43	Maintenance, Preventive Maintenance, Rebuilding, and Alteration
14 CFR part 61	Certification: Pilots and Flight Instructors
14 CFR part 67	Medical Standards and Certification
14 CFR part 91	General Operating and Flight Rules
NTSB part 830	Notification and Reporting of Aircraft Accidents and Incidents
FAA-H-8083-1	Aircraft Weight And Balance Handbook
FAA-H-8083-21	Rotorcraft Flying Handbook
FAA-H-8083-25	Pilot's Handbook of Aeronautical Knowledge
AC 00-6	Aviation Weather
AC 00-45	Aviation Weather Services
AC 60-22	Aeronautical Decision Making
AC 60-28	English Language Skill Standards Required by 14 CFR parts 61, 63, and 65
AC 61-65	Certification: Pilots and Flight Instructors and Ground Instructors
AC 61-84	Role of Preflight Preparation
AC 61-134	General Aviation Controlled Flight into Terrain Awareness
AC 90-48	Pilots' Role in Collision Avoidance
AC 90-87	Helicopter Dynamic Rollover
AC 90-95	Unanticipated right yaw in helicopters
AC 91-13	Cold Weather Operation of Aircraft
AC 91-32	Safety In and Around Helicopters
AC 91-42	Hazards of Rotating Propeller and Helicopter Rotor Blades
AC 91-55	Reduction of Electrical System failures following aircraft engine starting
AIM	Aeronautical Information Manual
AFD	Airport Facility Directory
FDC NOTAMs	National Flight data Center Notices to Airmen
Other	Pertinent Pilot's Operating Handbooks
	FAA-Approved Flight Manuals
	Navigation Charts

The Objective lists the important elements that must be satisfactorily performed to demonstrate competency in a TASK. The Objective includes:

1. specifically what the applicant should be able to do;
2. the conditions under which the TASK is to be performed; and
3. the acceptable standards of performance.

Abbreviations

14 CFR	Title 14 of the Code of Federal Regulations
ADM	Aeronautical Decision Making
AGL	Above Ground Level
ASOS	Automated Surface Observing System
ATC	Air Traffic Control
ATIS	Automatic Terminal Information Service
AWOS	Automated Weather Observing System
CFIT	Controlled Flight into Terrain
CG	Center of Gravity
CRM	Cockpit Resource Management
FA	Area Weather Forecast
FAA	Federal Aviation Administration
FDC	Flight Data Center
FSDO	Flight Standards District Office
GPO	Government Printing Office
ILS	Instrument Landing System
MEL	Minimum Equipment List
METAR	Aviation Routine Weather Report
NOTAM	Notice to Airmen
PTS	Practical Test Standard
RAIM	Receiver Autonomous Integrity Monitoring
RPM	Revolutions Per Minute
TAF	Terminal Aviation Forecast
VFR	Visual Flight Rules

Use Of The Practical Test Standards

The Commercial Pilot Rotorcraft Practical Test Standards have been designed to evaluate competency in both knowledge and skill. Commercial pilots are professionals engaged in various flight activities for compensation or hire. Because of their professional status, they should exhibit a significantly higher level of knowledge and skill than the private pilot. Although some TASKs listed are similar to those in the Private Pilot Rotorcraft Practical Test Standards, the wording used in the Commercial Pilot Rotorcraft Practical Test Standards reflects a higher level of competency expected of a commercial pilot applicant in performing these similar TASKs.

The FAA requires that all practical tests be conducted in accordance with the appropriate Commercial Pilot Practical Test Standards and the policies set forth in this INTRODUCTION. Commercial pilot applicants must be evaluated in **ALL** TASKs included in the AREAS OF OPERATION of the appropriate practical test standard unless otherwise noted.

An applicant, who holds at least a commercial pilot certificate seeking an additional rotorcraft category rating and/or class rating at the commercial pilot level will be evaluated in the AREAS OF OPERATION and TASKs listed in the Additional Rating Task Table. At the discretion of the examiner, an evaluation of the applicant's competence in the remaining AREAS OF OPERATION and TASKs may be conducted.

If the applicant holds two or more category or class ratings at least at the private level, and the Additional Rating Task Table indicates differing required TASKs, the "least restrictive" entry applies. For example, if "ALL" and "NONE" are indicated for one AREA OF OPERATION, the "NONE" entry applies. If "B" and "B, C" are indicated, the "B" entry applies.

In preparation for each practical test, the examiner must develop a written "plan of action." The "plan of action" is a tool, for the sole use of the examiner, to be used in evaluating the applicant. The plan of action need not be grammatically correct or in any formal format. The plan of action must contain all of the required AREAS OF OPERATION and TASKs and any optional TASKs selected by the examiner. The "plan of action" must incorporate one or more scenarios that will be used during the practical test.

The examiner should try to include as many of the TASKs into the scenario portion of the test as possible, but maintain the flexibility to change due to unexpected situations as they arise and still result in an efficient and valid test. *Any TASK selected for evaluation during a practical test is to be evaluated in its entirety.*

The examiner is not required to follow the precise order in which the AREAS OF OPERATION and TASKs appear in this book. The examiner may change the sequence or combine TASKs with similar objectives to have an orderly and efficient flow of the practical test. For example, lost procedures may be combined with radio navigation. The examiner's "plan of action" should include the order and combination of TASKs to be demonstrated by the applicant in a manner that will result in an efficient and valid test.

The examiner is expected to use good judgment in the performance of simulated emergency procedures. The use of the safest means for simulation is expected. Consideration must be given to local conditions (both meteorological and topographical), at the time of the test, as well as the applicant's, workload, and the condition of the aircraft used. If the procedure being evaluated would jeopardize safety, it is expected that the applicant will simulate that portion of the maneuver.

FAA-S-8081-16A

Special Emphasis Areas

Examiners must place special emphasis upon areas of aircraft operation considered critical to flight safety. Among these are:

1. positive aircraft control;
2. procedures for positive exchange of flight controls (who is flying the aircraft);
3. collision avoidance;
4. wake turbulence avoidance;
5. runway incursion avoidance;
6. CFIT;
7. wire strike avoidance;
8. ADM and risk management;
9. checklist usage; and
10. other areas deemed appropriate to any phase of the practical test.

Although these areas may not be specifically addressed under each TASK, they are essential to flight safety and will be evaluated during the practical test. In all instances, the applicant's actions will relate to the complete situation.

Commercial Pilot Rotorcraft Practical Test Prerequisites

An applicant for the Commercial Pilot Rotorcraft Practical Test is required by 14 CFR part 61 to:

1. possess a private pilot certificate or meets the flight experience required for a private pilot certificate and pass the private helicopter or gyroplane knowledge and practical test;
2. have passed the appropriate commercial pilot knowledge test since the beginning of the 24th month before the month in which the practical test is completed;
3. obtain the applicable instruction and aeronautical experience prescribed for the commercial pilot certificate or rating sought;
4. possess at least a current third-class medical certificate issued under 14 CFR part 67;
5. be at least 18 years of age;
6. obtain a written statement from an appropriately certificated flight instructor certifying that the applicant has been given flight instruction in preparation for the practical test within 60 days preceding the date of application. The statement must also state that the instructor finds the applicant competent to pass the practical test and that the applicant has satisfactory knowledge of the subject area(s) in which a deficiency was indicated by the airman knowledge test report; and
7. be able to read, speak, write, and understand the English language. If there is a doubt, use AC 60-28, English Language Skill Standards.

Aircraft And Equipment Required for the Practical Test

The commercial pilot applicant is required by 14 CFR part 61, section 61.45 to provide an airworthy, certificated aircraft for use during the practical test. This section further requires that the aircraft must:

1. be of U.S., foreign or military registry of the same category, class, and type, if applicable, for the certificate and/or rating for which the applicant is applying;
2. have fully functioning dual controls, except as provided in 14 CFR part 61, section 61.45(c) and (e); in this CFR section; and
3. be capable of performing ALL AREAS OF OPERATION appropriate to the rating sought and have no operating limitations, which prohibit its use in any of the AREAS OF OPERATION, required for the practical test.

Flight Instructor Responsibility

An appropriately rated flight instructor is responsible for training the commercial pilot applicant to acceptable standards in **ALL** subject matter areas, procedures, and maneuvers included in the TASKs within the appropriate commercial pilot practical test standard.

Because of the impact of their teaching activities in developing safe, proficient pilots, flight instructors should exhibit a high level of knowledge, skill, and the abilityto impart that knowledge and skill to students.

Throughout the applicant's training, the flight instructor is responsible for emphasizing the performance of effective visual scanning, collision avoidance, and runway incursion avoidance procedures.

Examiner Responsibility

The examiner conducting the practical test is responsible for determining that the applicant meets the acceptable standards of knowledge and skill of each TASK within the appropriate practical test standard. Since there is no formal division between the "oral" and "skill" portions of the practical test, this becomes an ongoing process throughout the test. To avoid unnecessary distractions, oral questioning, to determine the applicant's knowledge of TASKs and related safety factors, should be used judiciously at all times, especially during the flight portion of the practical test.

Examiners must test to the greatest extent practicable the applicant's correlative abilities rather than mere rote enumeration of facts throughout the practical test.

FAA-S-8081-16A

If the examiner determines that a TASK is incomplete, or the outcome uncertain, the examiner may require the applicant to repeat that TASK, or portions of that TASK. This provision has been made in the interest of fairness and does not mean that instruction, practice, or the repeating of an unsatisfactory TASK is permitted during the certification process.

Throughout the flight portion of the practical test, the examiner must evaluate the applicant's use of visual scanning and collision avoidance procedures.

Satisfactory Performance

Satisfactory performance to meet the requirements for certification is based on the applicant's ability to safely:

1. perform the TASKs specified in the AREAS OF OPERATION for the certificate or rating sought within the approved standards;
2. demonstrate mastery of the aircraft with the successful outcome of each TASK performed never seriously in doubt;
3. demonstrate satisfactory proficiency and competency within the approved standards;
4. demonstrate sound judgment and ADM; and
5. demonstrate single-pilot competence if the aircraft is type certificated for single-pilot operations.

Unsatisfactory Performance

The tolerances represent the performance expected in good flying conditions. If, in the judgment of the examiner, the applicant does not meet the standards of performance of any TASK performed, the associated AREA OF OPERATION is failed and therefore, the practical test is failed.

The examiner or applicant may discontinue the test at any time when the failure of an AREA OF OPERATION makes the applicant ineligible for the certificate or rating sought. *The test may be continued ONLY with the consent of the applicant*. If the test is discontinued, the applicant is entitled credit for only those AREAS OF OPERATION and their associated TASKs satisfactorily performed. However, during the retest and at the discretion of the examiner, any TASK may be re-evaluated including those previously passed.

Typical areas of unsatisfactory performance and grounds for disqualification are:

1. Any action or lack of action by the applicant that requires corrective intervention by the examiner to maintain safe flight.
2. Failure to use proper and effective visual scanning techniques to clear the area before and while performing maneuvers.
3. Consistently exceeding tolerances stated in the Objectives.
4. Failure to take prompt corrective action when tolerances are exceeded.

When a Notice of Disapproval is issued, the examiner will record the applicant's unsatisfactory performance and TASK(s) not completed in terms of AREA OF OPERATION(s) and specific TASK(s) not meeting the standard appropriate to the practical test conducted. The AREA(s) OF OPERATION/TASK(s) not tested and the number of practical test failures must also be recorded. If the applicant fails the practical test because of a special emphasis area, the Notice of Disapproval must indicate the associated TASK. i.e.: AREA OF OPERATION VIII, Settling-With-Power, failure to use proper collision avoidance procedures.

Letter of Discontinuance

When a practical test is discontinued for reasons other than unsatisfactory performance (i.e., equipment failure, weather, or illness) FAA Form 8700-1, Airman Certificate and/or Rating Application, and, if applicable, the Airman Knowledge Test Report, is to be returned to the applicant. The examiner at that time prepares, signs, and issues a Letter of Discontinuance to the applicant. The Letter of Discontinuance should identify the AREAS OF OPERATION and their associated TASKs of the practical test that were successfully completed. The applicant should be advised that the Letter of Discontinuance must be presented to the examiner when the practical test is resumed, and made part of the certification file.

Aeronautical Decision Making and Risk Management

Throughout the practical test, the examiner evaluates the applicant's ability to use good aeronautical decision-making procedures in order to identify risks. The examiner accomplishes this requirement by developing scenarios that incorporate as many TASKs as possible to evaluate the applicants risk management in making safe aeronautical decisions. For example, the examiner may develop a scenario that incorporates weather decisions and performance planning.

The applicant's ability to utilize all the assets available in making a risk analysis to determine the safest course of action is essential for satisfactory performance. The scenarios should be realistic and within the capabilities of the aircraft used for the practical test.

Single-Pilot Resource Management

Single-pilot resource management refers to the effective use of ALL available resources: human resources, hardware, and information. It is similar to crew resource management (CRM) procedures that are being emphasized in multi-crewmember operations except that only one crewmember (the pilot) is involved. Human resources "...includes all other groups routinely working with the pilot who are involved in decisions that are required to operate a flight safely. These groups include, but are not limited to: dispatchers, weather briefers, maintenance personnel, and air traffic controllers." Pilot resource management is not a single TASK; it is a set of skill competencies that must be evident in all TASKs in this practical test standard as applied to single-pilot operation.

Applicant's Use of Checklists

Throughout the practical test, the applicant is evaluated on the use of an appropriate checklist. Proper use is dependent on the specific TASK being evaluated. The situation may be such that the use of the checklist while accomplishing the elements of the Objective would be either unsafe or impractical, especially in a single-pilot operation. In this case, a review of the checklist after the elements have been accomplished would be appropriate. Division of attention and proper visual scanning would be considered when using a checklist.

Use Of Distractions During Practical Tests

Numerous studies indicate that many accidents have occurred when the pilot has been distracted during critical phases of flight. To evaluate the pilot's ability to utilize proper control technique while dividing attention both inside and/or outside the cockpit, the examiner should cause a realistic distraction during the **flight** portion of the practical test to evaluate the applicant's ability to divide attention while maintaining safe flight.

Positive Exchange of Flight Controls

During flight, there must always be a clear understanding between pilots of who has control of the aircraft. Prior to flight, a briefing should be conducted that includes the procedure for the exchange of flight controls. A positive three-step process in the exchange of flight controls between pilots is a proven procedure and one that is strongly recommended.

When one pilot wishes to give the other pilot control of the aircraft, he or she will say, "You have the flight controls." The other pilot acknowledges immediately by saying, "I have the flight controls." The first pilot again says, "You have the flight controls." When control is returned to the first pilot, follow the same procedure. A visual check is recommended to verify that the exchange has occurred. There should never be any doubt as to who is flying the aircraft.

SECTION 1

COMMERCIAL PILOT
ROTORCRAFT — HELICOPTER

CONTENTS: SECTION 1

ADDITIONAL RATING TASK TABLE

Addition of a Rotorcraft/Helicopter rating to an existing Commercial Pilot Certificate

Required TASKs are indicated by either the TASK letter(s) that apply(s) or an indication that all or none of the TASKs must be tested based on the notes in each AREA OF OPERATION.

COMMERCIAL PILOT RATING(S) HELD

AREAS OF OPER- ATION	ASEL	ASES	AMEL	AMES	RG	Glider	Balloon	Airship
I	F,G,I,J	F,G,I,J	F,G,I,J	F,G,I,J	F,G,I,J	F,G,I,J	F,G,I,J	F,G,I,J
II	ALL	ALL	ALL	ALL	ALL	ALL	ALL	ALL
III	B,C	B,C	B,C	B,C	ALL	ALL	ALL	B,C
IV	ALL	ALL	ALL	ALL	ALL	ALL	ALL	ALL
V	ALL	ALL	ALL	ALL	ALL	ALL	ALL	ALL
VI	ALL	ALL	ALL	ALL	ALL	ALL	ALL	ALL
VII	NONE	NONE	NONE	NONE	B	B,C,D	B,C,D	NONE
VIII	ALL	ALL	ALL	ALL	ALL	ALL	ALL	ALL
IX	ALL	ALL	ALL	ALL	ALL	ALL	ALL	ALL
X	ALL	ALL	ALL	ALL	ALL	ALL	ALL	ALL

FAA-S-8081-16A

APPLICANT'S PRACTICAL TEST CHECKLIST
(HELICOPTER)
APPOINTMENT WITH EXAMINER:

EXAMINER'S NAME_____

LOCATION _____

DATE/TIME _____

ACCEPTABLE AIRCRAFT

- ☐ Aircraft Documents:
    Airworthiness Certificate
    Registration Certificate
    Operating Limitations
- ☐ Aircraft Maintenance Records:
    Logbook Record of Airworthiness Inspections
    and AD Compliance
- ☐ Pilot's Operating Handbook and FAA-Approved
    Helicopter Flight Manual
- ☐ FCC Station License

PERSONAL EQUIPMENT

- ☐ View-Limiting Device
- ☐ Current Aeronautical Charts
- ☐ Computer and Plotter
- ☐ Flight Plan Form
- ☐ Flight Logs
- ☐ Current AIM, Airport Facility Directory, and Appropriate
    Publications

PERSONAL RECORDS

- ☐ Identification - Photo/Signature ID
- ☐ Pilot Certificate
- ☐ Current and Appropriate Medical Certificate
- ☐ Completed FAA Form 8710-1, Airman Certificate and/or
    Rating Application with Instructor's Signature (if
    applicable)
- ☐ AC Form 8080-2, Airman Written Test Report, or
    Computer Test Report
- ☐ Pilot Logbook with Appropriate Instructor Endorsements
- ☐ FAA Form 8060-5, Notice of Disapproval (if applicable)
- ☐ Approved School Graduation Certificate (if applicable)
- ☐ Examiner's Fee (if applicable)

EXAMINER'S PRACTICAL TEST CHECKLIST

(HELICOPTER)

APPLICANT'S NAME_____

LOCATION_____

DATE/TIME_____

I. PREFLIGHT PREPARATION

- ☐ **A.** CERTIFICATES AND DOCUMENTS
- ☐ **B.** AIRWORTHINESS REQUIREMENTS
- ☐ **C.** WEATHER INFORMATION
- ☐ **D.** CROSS-COUNTRY FLIGHT PLANNING
- ☐ **E.** NATIONAL AIRSPACE SYSTEM
- ☐ **F.** PERFORMANCE AND LIMITATIONS
- ☐ **G.** OPERATION OF SYSTEMS
- ☐ **H.** AEROMEDICAL FACTORS
- ☐ **I.** PHYSIOLOGICAL ASPECTS OF NIGHT FLYING
- ☐ **J.** LIGHTING AND EQUIPMENT FOR NIGHT FLYING

II. PREFLIGHT PROCEDURES

- ☐ **A.** PREFLIGHT INSPECTION
- ☐ **B.** COCKPIT MANAGEMENT
- ☐ **C.** ENGINE STARTING AND ROTOR ENGAGEMENT
- ☐ **D.** BEFORE TAKEOFF CHECK

III. AIRPORT AND HELIPORT OPERATIONS

- ☐ **A.** RADIO COMMUNICATIONS AND ATC LIGHT SIGNALS
- ☐ **B.** TRAFFIC PATTERNS
- ☐ **C.** AIRPORT/HELIPORT RUNWAY, HELIPORT, AND TAXIWAY SIGNS, MARKINGS, AND LIGHTING

IV. HOVERING MANEUVERS

- ☐ **A.** VERTICAL TAKEOFF AND LANDING
- ☐ **B.** SLOPE OPERATIONS
- ☐ **C.** SURFACE TAXI
- ☐ **D.** HOVER TAXI
- ☐ **E.** AIR TAXI

FAA-S-8081-16A

V. TAKEOFFS, LANDINGS, AND GO-AROUNDS

- [ ] **A.** NORMAL AND CROSSWIND TAKEOFF AND CLIMB
- [ ] **B.** NORMAL AND CROSSWIND APPROACH
- [ ] **C.** MAXIMUM PERFORMANCE TAKEOFF AND CLIMB
- [ ] **D.** STEEP APPROACH
- [ ] **E.** ROLLING TAKEOFF
- [ ] **F.** SHALLOW APPROACH AND RUNNING/ROLL-ON LANDING
- [ ] **G.** GO-AROUND

VI. PERFORMANCE MANEUVERS

- [ ] **A.** RAPID DECELERATION
- [ ] **B.** STRAIGHT IN ADUTOROTATION
- [ ] **C.** 180° AUTOROTATION
- [ ] **D.** APPROACH AND LANDING WITH SIMULATED POWERPLANT FAILURE – MULTIENGINE HELICOPTER

VII. NAVIGATION

- [ ] **A.** PILOTAGE AND DEAD RECKONING
- [ ] **B.** RADIO NAVIGATION AND RADAR SERVICES
- [ ] **C.** DIVERSION
- [ ] **D.** LOST PROCEDURES

VIII. EMERGENCY OPERATIONS

- [ ] **A.** POWER FAILURE AT A HOVER
- [ ] **B.** POWER FAILURE AT ALTITUDE
- [ ] **C.** SYSTEMS AND EQUIPMENT MALFUNCTIONS
- [ ] **D.** SETTLING-WITH-POWER
- [ ] **E.** LOW ROTOR RPM RECOVERY
- [ ] **F.** DYNAMIC ROLLOVER
- [ ] **G.** GROUND RESONANCE
- [ ] **H.** LOW G CONDITIONS
- [ ] **I.** EMERGENCY EQUIPMENT AND SURVIVAL GEAR

IX. SPECIAL OPERATIONS

- [ ] **A.** CONFINED AREA OPERATION
- [ ] **B.** PINNACLE/PLATFORM OPERATIONS

X. POST-FLIGHT PROCEDURES

- [ ] AFTER LANDING AND SECURING

I. AREA OF OPERATION: PREFLIGHT PREPARATION

A. TASK: CERTIFICATES AND DOCUMENTS

REFERENCE(S): 14 CFR parts 43, 61, 67, 91; FAA-H-8083-21, FAA-H-8083-25; POH/RFM.

Objective. To determine that the applicant exhibits knowledge of the elements related to certificates and documents by:

1. Explaining—

   a. commercial pilot certificate privileges, limitations, and recent flight experience requirements.
   b. medical certificate class and duration.
   c. pilot logbook or flight records.

2. Locating and explaining—

   a. airworthiness and registration certificates.
   b. operating limitations, placards, POH/RFM, and instrument markings.
   c. weight and balance data and equipment list.

B. TASK: AIRWORTHINESS REQUIREMENTS

REFERENCE(S): 14 CFR part 91; FAA-H-8083-21.

Objective. To determine that the applicant exhibits knowledge of the elements related to airworthiness requirements by:

1. Explaining—

   a. required instruments and equipment for day/night VFR.
   b. procedures and limitations for determining airworthiness of the helicopter with inoperative instruments and equipment with and without an MEL.
   c. requirements and procedures for obtaining a special flight permit.

2. Locating and explaining—

   a. airworthiness directives.
   b. compliance records.
   c. maintenance/inspection requirements.
   d. appropriate record keeping.

C. TASK: WEATHER INFORMATION

REFERENCE(S): AC 00-6, AC 00-45, AC 61-84; FAA-H-8083-25; AIM.

Objective. To determine that the applicant:

1. Exhibits knowledge of the elements related to weather information by analyzing available weather reports, charts, and forecasts from various sources with emphasis on—

   a. METAR, TAF, and FA.
   b. surface analysis chart.
   c. wind shear reports.
   d. winds and temperature aloft chart.
   e. AWOS, ASOS, and ATIS reports.
   f. significant weather prognostic charts.

2. Makes a competent "go/no-go" decision based on available weather information.

D. TASK: CROSS-COUNTRY FLIGHT PLANNING

REFERENCE(S): AC 61-84; FAA-H-8083-25; Navigation Charts; Airport/Facility Directory; FDC NOTAMs; AIM.

NOTE: In-flight demonstration of cross-country procedures by the applicant is tested under AREA OF OPERATION: NAVIGATION.

Objective. To determine that the applicant:

1. Exhibits knowledge of the elements related to cross-country flight planning by presenting and explaining a pre-planned VFR cross-country flight, as previously assigned by the examiner. On the day of the practical test, the flight plan should be to the first fuel stop necessary, based on maximum allowable passenger, baggage, and/or cargo loads using real-time weather.
2. Uses appropriate and current aeronautical charts.
3. Properly identifies airspace, obstructions, and terrain features, including discussion of wire strike avoidance techniques.
4. Selects easily identifiable en route checkpoints.
5. Selects most favorable altitudes, considering weather conditions and equipment capabilities.
6. Computes headings, flight time, and fuel requirements.
7. Selects appropriate navigation systems/facilities and communication frequencies.
8. Extracts and applies pertinent information from NOTAMs, Airport/Facility Directory, and other flight publications.
9. Completes a navigation log and simulates filing a VFR flight plan.

E. TASK: NATIONAL AIRSPACE SYSTEM

REFERENCE(S): 14 CFR parts 71, 91; Navigation Charts; AIM.

Objective. To determine that the applicant exhibits knowledge of the elements related to the national airspace system by explaining:

1. Basic VFR Weather Minimums – for all classes of airspace.
2. Airspace classes – their operating rules, pilot certification, and helicopter equipment requirements for the following—

   a. Class A.
   b. Class B.
   c. Class C.
   d. Class D.
   e. Class E.
   f. Class G.

3. Special use airspace and other airspace areas.

F. TASK: PERFORMANCE AND LIMITATIONS

REFERENCE(S): FAA-H-8083-1, FAA-H-8083-21; AC 91-23; POH/RFM.

Objective. To determine that the applicant:

1. Exhibits knowledge of the elements related to performance and limitations by explaining the use of charts, tables, and data to determine performance and the adverse effects of exceeding limitations.
2. Computes weight and balance. Determines the computed weight and center of gravity is within the helicopter's operating limitations and if the center of gravity will remain within limits during all phases of flight.
3. Demonstrates the use of appropriate performance charts, tables, and data.
4. Describes the effects of various atmospheric conditions on the helicopter's performance.
5. Understands the cause and effects of retreating blade stall.
6. Considers circumstances when operating within " avoid areas" of the height/velocity diagram.
7. Is aware of situations that lead to loss of tail rotor/antitorque effectiveness (unanticipated yaw).

G. TASK: OPERATION OF SYSTEMS

REFERENCE(S): FAA-H-8083-21; POH/AFM.

Objective. To determine that the applicant exhibits knowledge of the elements related to the appropriate normal operating procedures and limitations of the following systems by explaining:

1. Primary flight controls, trim, and, if installed, stability control.
2. Powerplant.
3. Main rotor and antitorque.
4. Landing gear, brakes, steering, skids, or floats, as applicable.
5. Fuel, oil, and hydraulic.
6. Electrical.
7. Pitot-static, vacuum/pressure and associated flight instruments, if applicable.
8. Environmental.
9. Anti-icing, including carburetor heat, if applicable.
10. Avionics equipment.

H. TASK: AEROMEDICAL FACTORS

REFERENCE(S): FAA-H-8083-25; AIM.

Objective. To determine that the applicant exhibits knowledge of the elements related to aeromedical factors by explaining:

1. The symptoms, causes, effects, and corrective actions of at least three (3) of the following—

   a. hypoxia.
   b. hyperventilation.
   c. middle ear and sinus problems.
   d. spatial disorientation.
   e. motion sickness.
   f. carbon monoxide poisoning.
   g. stress and fatigue.
   h. dehydration.

2. The effects of alcohol and drugs, including over-the-counter drugs.
3. The effects of nitrogen excesses during scuba dives upon a pilot and/or passenger in flight.

I. TASK: PHYSIOLOGICAL ASPECTS OF NIGHT FLYING

REFERENCE(S):   FAA-H-8083-21, FAA-H-8083-25; AIM.

Objective.   To determine that the applicant exhibits knowledge of the elements related to the physiological aspects of night flying by explaining:

1. The function of various parts of the eye essential for night vision.
2. Adaptation of the eye to changing light.
3. Correct use of the eye to accommodate changing light.
4. Coping with illusions created by various light conditions.
5. Effects of the pilot's physical condition on visual acuity.
6. Methods for increasing vision effectiveness.

J. TASK: LIGHTING AND EQUIPMENT FOR NIGHT FLYING

REFERENCE(S):   FAA-H-8083-21, FAA-H-8083-25; POH/RFM.

Objective.   To determine that the applicant:

1. Exhibits knowledge of the elements related to lighting and equipment for night flying by explaining—

   a. the types and uses of various personal lighting devices.
   b. the required equipment, and location of external navigation lighting of the helicopter.
   c. the meaning of various airport, heliport, and navigation lights, the method of determining their status, and the procedure for airborne activation of runway lights.

2. Locates and identifies switches, spare fuses, and circuit breakers pertinent to night operations.

II. AREA OF OPERATION: PREFLIGHT PROCEDURES

A. TASK: PREFLIGHT INSPECTION

REFERENCE(S): FAA-H-8083-21; POH/RFM.

Objective. To determine that the applicant:

1. Exhibits knowledge of the elements related to a preflight inspection. Including, which items must be inspected, the reasons for checking each item, and how to detect possible defects.
2. Inspects the helicopter with reference to an appropriate checklist.
3. Verifies that the helicopter is in condition for safe flight.

B. TASK: COCKPIT MANAGEMENT

REFERENCE(S): 14 CFR part 91; AC 91-32; POH/RFM.

Objective. To determine that the applicant:

1. Exhibits knowledge of the elements related to cockpit management procedures.
2. Ensures all loose items in the cockpit and cabin are secured.
3. Organizes material and equipment in an efficient manner so they are readily available.
4. Briefs the occupants on the use of safety belts, shoulder harnesses, doors, rotor blade avoidance, and emergency procedures.

C. TASK: ENGINE STARTING AND ROTOR ENGAGEMENT

REFERENCE(S): FAA-H-8083-21; AC 91-13, AC 91-42, AC 91-55; POH/RFM.

Objective. To determine that the applicant:

1. Exhibits knowledge of the elements related to correct engine starting procedures. Including, the use of an external power source, starting under various atmospheric conditions, awareness of other persons and property during start, and the effects of using incorrect starting procedures.
2. Ensures proper rotor blade clearance, and frictions flight controls, as necessary.
3. Utilizes the appropriate checklist for starting procedures.

D. TASK: BEFORE TAKEOFF CHECK

REFERENCE(S):   FAA-H-8083-21; POH/RFM.

Objective.   To determine that the applicant:

1. Exhibits knowledge of the elements related to the before takeoff check. Including, the reasons for checking each item and how to detect malfunctions.
2. Positions the helicopter properly considering other aircraft, wind, and surface conditions.
3. Divides attention inside and outside the cockpit.
4. Ensures that the engine temperature and pressure are suitable for run-up and takeoff.
5. Accomplishes the before takeoff check and ensures that the helicopter is in safe operating condition.
6. Reviews takeoff performance airspeeds, takeoff distances, departure, and emergency procedures.
7. Avoids runway incursions and/or ensures no conflict with traffic prior to takeoff.

III. AREA OF OPERATION: AIRPORT AND HELIPORT OPERATIONS

A. TASK: RADIO COMMUNICATIONS AND ATC LIGHT SIGNALS

REFERENCE(S): 14 CFR part 91; FAA-H-8083-25; AIM.

Objective. To determine that the applicant:

1. Exhibits knowledge of the elements related to radio communications and ATC light signals.
2. Selects appropriate frequencies.
3. Transmits using recommended phraseology.
4. Acknowledges radio communications and complies with instructions.

B. TASK: TRAFFIC PATTERNS

REFERENCE(S): 14 CFR part 91; FAA-H-8083-21; AIM, POH/RFM.

Objective. To determine that the applicant:

1. Exhibits knowledge of the elements related to traffic patterns. Including, procedures at airports and heliports with and without operating control towers, prevention of runway incursions collision avoidance, wake turbulence avoidance, and wind shear.
2. Complies with proper traffic pattern procedures.
3. Maintains proper spacing from other traffic or avoids the flow of fixed wing aircraft.
4. Corrects for wind drift to maintain proper ground track.
5. Maintains orientation with runway/landing area.
6. Maintains traffic pattern altitude ±100 feet, and appropriate airspeed, ±10 knots.

C. TASK: AIRPORT/HELIPORT RUNWAY, HELIPAD, AND TAXIWAY SIGNS, MARKINGS, AND LIGHTING

REFERENCE(S): 14 CFR part 91; FAA-H-8083-25; AIM.

Objective. To determine that the applicant:

1. Exhibits knowledge of the elements related to airport/heliport runway, and taxiway operations with emphasis on runway incursion avoidance.
2. Properly identifies and interprets airport/heliport, runway, and taxiway signs, markings, and lighting.

IV. AREA OF OPERATION: HOVERING MANEUVERS

A. TASK: VERTICAL TAKEOFF AND LANDING

REFERENCE(S):   FAA-H-8083-21; AC 90-95; POH/RFM.

Objective. To determine that the applicant:

1. Exhibits knowledge of the elements related to a vertical takeoff to a hover and landing from a hover.
2. Ascends to and maintains recommended hovering altitude, and descends from recommended hovering altitude in headwind, crosswind, and tailwind conditions.
3. Maintains RPM within normal limits.
4. Establishes recommended hovering altitude, ±1/2 of that altitude within 10 feet of the surface; if above 10 feet, ±5 feet.
5. Avoids conditions that might lead to loss of tail rotor/antitorque effectiveness.
6. Keeps forward and sideward movement within 2 feet of a designated point, with no aft movement.
7. Descends vertically to within 2 feet of the designated touchdown point.
8. Maintains specified heading, ±10°.

B. TASK: SLOPE OPERATIONS

REFERENCE(S):   FAA-H-8083-21; POH/RFM.

Objective.   To determine that the applicant:

1. Exhibits knowledge of the elements related to slope operations.
2. Selects a suitable slope, approach, and direction considering wind effect, obstacles, dynamic rollover avoidance, and discharging passengers.
3. Properly moves toward the slope.
4. Maintains RPM within normal limits.
5. Makes a smooth positive descent to touch the upslope skid on the sloping surface.
6. Maintains positive control while lowering the downslope skid or landing gear to touchdown.
7. Recognizes when the slope is too steep and abandons the operation prior to reaching cyclic control stops.
8. Makes a smooth transition from the slope to a stabilized hover parallel to the slope.
9. Properly moves away from the slope.
10. Maintains the specified heading throughout the operation, ±5°.

C. TASK: SURFACE TAXI

REFERENCE(S): FAA-H-8083-21; AIM, POH/AFM.

NOTE: This TASK applies to only helicopters equipped with wheel-type landing gear.

Objective. To determine that the applicant:

1. Exhibits knowledge of the elements related to surface taxiing.
2. Surface taxies the helicopter from one point to another under headwind, crosswind, and tailwind conditions, with the landing gear in contact with the surface, avoiding conditions that might lead to loss of tail rotor/antitorque effectiveness.
3. Properly uses cyclic, collective, and brakes to control speed while taxiing.
4. Properly positions nosewheel/tailwheel, if applicable, locked or unlocked.
5. Maintains RPM within normal limits.
6. Maintains appropriate speed for existing conditions.
7. Stops helicopter within ± 2 feet of a specified point.
8. Maintains specified track within ± 2 feet.

D. TASK: HOVER TAXI

REFERENCE(S): FAA-H-8083-21; AIM; POH/RFM.

Objective. To determine that the applicant:

1. Exhibits knowledge of the elements related to hover taxiing.
2. Hover taxies over specified ground references, demonstrating forward, sideward, and rearward hovering and hovering turns.
3. Maintains RPM within normal limits.
4. Maintains specified ground track within ± 2 feet on straight legs.
5. Maintains constant rate of turn at pivot points.
6. Maintains position within ± 2 feet of each pivot point during turns.
7. Makes 90°, 180°, and 360° pivoting turns, stopping within 10° of specified headings.
8. Maintains recommended hovering altitude, ±1/2 of that altitude within 10 feet of the surface, if above 10 feet, ±5 feet.

E. TASK: AIR TAXI

REFERENCE(S):   FAA-H-8083-21; AC 90-95; AIM; POH/RFM.

Objective.   To determine that the applicant:

1. Exhibits knowledge of the elements related to air taxiing.
2. Air taxies the helicopter from one point to another under headwind and crosswind conditions.
3. Maintains RPM within normal limits.
4. Selects a safe airspeed and altitude.
5. Maintains desired track and groundspeed in headwind and crosswind conditions, avoiding conditions that might lead to loss of tail rotor/antitorque effectiveness.
6. Maintains a specified altitude, ±5 feet.

V. AREA OF OPERATION: TAKEOFFS, LANDINGS, AND GO-AROUNDS

A. TASK: NORMAL AND CROSSWIND TAKEOFF AND CLIMB

REFERENCE(S): FAA-H-8083-21; POH/RFM.

NOTE: If a calm wind weather condition exists, the applicant's knowledge of the crosswind elements must be evaluated through oral testing; otherwise a crosswind takeoff and climb must be demonstrated.

Objective. To determine that the applicant:

1. Exhibits knowledge of the elements related to normal and crosswind takeoff and climb, including factors affecting performance, to include height/velocity information.
2. Establishes a stationary position on the surface or a stabilized hover, prior to takeoff in headwind and crosswind conditions.
3. Maintains RPM within normal limits.
4. Accelerates to manufacturer's recommended climb airspeed, ±5 knots.
5. Maintains proper ground track with crosswind correction, as necessary.
6. Remains aware of the possibility of wind shear and/or wake turbulence.

B. TASK: NORMAL AND CROSSWIND APPROACH

REFERENCE(S):   FAA-H-8083-21; POH/RFM.

NOTE: If a calm wind weather condition exists, the applicant's knowledge of the crosswind elements must be evaluated through oral testing; otherwise a crosswind approach and landing must be demonstrated.

Objective.   To determine that the applicant:

1. Exhibits knowledge of the elements related to normal and crosswind approach.
2. Considers performance data, to include height/velocity information.
3. Considers the wind conditions, landing surface, and obstacles.
4. Selects a suitable termination point.
5. Establishes and maintains the normal approach angle, and rate of closure.
6. Remains aware of the possibility of wind shear and/or wake turbulence.
7. Avoids situations that may result in settling-with-power.
8. Maintains proper ground track with crosswind correction, as necessary.
9. Arrives at the termination point, on the surface or at a stabilized hover, ±2 feet.

C. TASK: MAXIMUM PERFORMANCE TAKEOFF AND CLIMB

REFERENCE(S):   FAA-H-8083-21; POH/RFM.

Objective.   To determine that the applicant:

1. Exhibits knowledge of the elements related to maximum performance takeoff and climb.
2. Considers situations where this maneuver is recommended and factors related to takeoff and climb performance, to include height/velocity information.
3. Maintains RPM within normal limits.
4. Utilizes proper control technique to initiate takeoff and forward climb airspeed attitude.
5. Utilizes the maximum available takeoff power.
6. After clearing all obstacles, transitions to normal climb attitude, airspeed, ±5 knots, and power setting.
7. Remains aware of the possibility of wind shear and/or wake turbulence.
8. Maintains proper ground track with crosswind correction, as necessary.

D. TASK: STEEP APPROACH

REFERENCE(S):   FAA-H-8083-21; POH/RFM.

Objective.   To determine that the applicant:

1. Exhibits knowledge of the elements related to a steep approach.
2. Considers situations where this maneuver is recommended and factors related to a steep approach, to include height/velocity information.
3. Considers the wind conditions, landing surface, and obstacles.
4. Selects a suitable termination point.
5. Establishes and maintains the recommended approach angle, (15° maximum) and proper rate of closure.
6. Avoids situations that can result in settling-with-power.
7. Remains aware of the possibility of wind shear and/or wake turbulence.
8. Maintains proper ground track with crosswind correction, if necessary.
9. Arrives at the termination point, on the surface or at a stabilized hover, ±2 feet.

E. TASK: ROLLING TAKEOFF

REFERENCE(S):   FAA-H-8083-21; POH/RFM.

NOTE: This TASK applies only to helicopters equipped with wheel-type landing gear.

Objective. To determine that the applicant:

1. Exhibits knowledge of the elements related to a rolling takeoff.
2. Considers situations where this maneuver is recommended and factors related to takeoff and climb performance, to include height/velocity information.
3. Maintains RPM within normal limits.
4. Utilizes proper preparatory technique prior to initiating takeoff.
5. Initiates forward accelerating movement on the surface.
6. Transitions to a normal climb airspeed, ±5 knots, and power setting.
7. Remains aware of the possibility of wind shear and/or wake turbulence.
8. Maintains proper ground track with crosswind correction, if necessary.
9. Completes the prescribed checklist, if applicable.

F. TASK: SHALLOW APPROACH AND RUNNING/ROLL-ON LANDING

REFERENCE(S): FAA-H-8083-21; POH/RFM.

Objective. To determine that the applicant:

1. Exhibits knowledge of the elements related to shallow approach and running/roll-on landing, including the purpose of the maneuver, factors affecting performance data, to include height/velocity information, and effect of landing surface texture.
2. Maintains RPM within normal limits.
3. Considers obstacles and other hazards.
4. Establishes and maintains the recommended approach angle, and proper rate of closure.
5. Remains aware of the possibility of wind shear and/or wake turbulence.
6. Maintains proper ground track with crosswind correction, if necessary.
7. Maintains a speed that will take advantage of effective translational lift during surface contact with landing gear parallel with the ground track.
8. Utilizes proper flight control technique after surface contact.
9. Completes the prescribed checklist, if applicable.

G. TASK: GO-AROUND

REFERENCE(S): FAA-H-8083-21; POH/AFM.

Objective. To determine that the applicant:

1. Exhibits knowledge of the elements related to a go-around and when it is necessary.
2. Makes a timely decision to discontinue the approach to landing.
3. Maintains RPM within normal limits.
4. Establishes proper control input to stop descent and initiate climb.
5. Retracts the landing gear, if applicable, after a positive rate of climb indication.
6. Maintains proper ground track with crosswind correction, if necessary.
7. Transitions to a normal climb airspeed, ±5 knots.
8. Completes the prescribed checklist, if applicable.

VI. AREA OF OPERATION: PERFORMANCE MANEUVERS

NOTE: The examiner must select TASK A and at least one other TASK.

A. TASK: RAPID DECELERATION

REFERENCE(S):   FAA-H-8083-21; Helicopter Flight Manual.

Objective.   To determine that the applicant:

1. Exhibits knowledge of the elements related to rapid deceleration.
2. Maintains RPM within normal limits.
3. Properly coordinates all controls throughout the execution of the maneuver.
4. Maintains an altitude that will permit safe clearance between the tail boom and the surface.
5. Decelerates and terminates in a stationary hover at the recommended hovering altitude.
6. Maintains heading throughout the maneuver, ±5°.

B. TASK: STRAIGHT IN AUTOROTATION

REFERENCE(S):   FAA-H-8083-21; POH/RFM.

Objective.   To determine that the applicant:

1. Exhibits knowledge of the elements related to a straight in autorotation terminating with a power recovery to a hover.
2. Selects a suitable touchdown area.
3. Initiates the maneuver at the proper point.
4. Establishes proper aircraft trim and autorotation airspeed, ± 5 knots.
5. Maintains rotor RPM within normal limits.
6. Compensates for windspeed and direction as necessary to void undershooting or overshooting the selected landing area.
7. Utilizes proper deceleration, collective pitch application to a hover.
8. Comes to a hover within 100 feet of a designated point.

C. TASK: 180° AUTOROTATION

REFERENCE(S): FAA-H-8083-21; POH/RFM.

Objective. To determine that the applicant:

1. Exhibits knowledge of the elements related to a 180° autorotation terminating with a power recovery to a hover.
2. Selects a suitable touchdown area.
3. Initiates the maneuver at the proper point.
4. Establishes proper aircraft trim and autorotation airspeed, ±5 knots.
5. Maintains rotor RPM within normal limits.
6. Compensates for windspeed and direction as necessary to avoid undershooting or overshooting the selected landing area.
7. Utilizes proper deceleration, collective pitch application to a hover.
8. Comes to a hover within 100 feet of a designated point.

D. TASK: APPROACH AND LANDING WITH SIMULATED POWERPLANT FAILURE - MULTIENGINE HELICOPER

REFERENCE(S): FAA-H-8083-21; POH/RFM.

NOTE: In a multiengine helicopter maneuvering to a landing, the applicant should follow a procedure that simulates the loss of one powerplant.

Objective. To determine that the applicant:

1. Exhibits adequate knowledge of maneuvering to a landing with a powerplant inoperative, including the controllability factors associated with maneuvering, and the applicable emergency procedures.
2. Selects a suitable touchdown point.
3. Maintains, prior to beginning the final approach segment, the desired altitude ± 100 feet, the desired airspeed ± 10 knots, the desired heading ± 5° , and maintains desired track.
4. Establishes the approach and landing configuration appropriate for the runway or landing area, and adjusts the powerplant controls as required.
5. Maintains a normal approach angle and recommended airspeed to the point of transition to touchdown.
6. Terminates the approach in a smooth transition to touchdown.
7. Completes the after-landing checklist items in a timely manner, after clearing the landing area, and as recommended by the manufacturer.

VII.   AREA OF OPERATION: NAVIGATION

A. TASK: PILOTAGE AND DEAD RECKONING

REFERENCE(S):   FAA-H-8083-25; AC 61-84.

Objective.   To determine that the applicant:

1. Exhibits knowledge of the elements related to pilotage and dead reckoning.
2. Follows the preplanned course by reference to landmarks.
3. Identifies landmarks by relating the surface features to chart symbols.
4. Navigates by means of precomputed headings, groundspeeds, and elapsed time.
5. Corrects for, and records, the differences between preflight fuel, groundspeed, and heading calculations and those determined en route.
6. Verifies the helicopter's position within three (3) nautical miles of the flight planned route.
7. Corrects for, and records, the differences between preflight fuel, groundspeed, and heading calculations and those determined en route.
8. Maintains the appropriate altitude, ±100 feet and established heading, ±10°.

B. TASK: RADIO NAVIGATION AND RADAR SERVICES

REFERENCE(S):   FAA-H-8083-25; AC 61-84;   Navigation Equipment Operation Manuals.

Objective.   To determine that the applicant:

1. Exhibits knowledge of the elements related to radio navigation and ATC radar services.
2. Selects and identifies the appropriate facilities or coordinates, as appropriate.
3. Locates the helicopter's position relative to the navigation facilities or coordinates, as appropriate.
4. Intercepts and tracks a given radial or bearing.
5. Locates position using cross radials, coordinates, or bearings.
6. Recognizes and describes the indication of station or way point passage.
7. Recognizes signal loss and takes appropriate action.
8. Uses proper communication procedures when utilizing ATC radar services.
9. Maintains the appropriate altitude, ±100 feet.

C. TASK: DIVERSION

REFERENCE(S):   FAA-H-8083-21; FAA-H-8083-25; AIM.

Objective.   To determine that the applicant:

1. Exhibits knowledge of the elements related to procedures for diversion.
2. Selects an appropriate alternate airport or heliport and route.
3. Promptly, diverts toward the alternate airport or heliport.
4. Makes an accurate estimate of heading, groundspeed, arrival time, and fuel consumption to the alternate airport or heliport.
5. Maintains the appropriate altitude, ±100 feet and established heading, ±10°.

D. TASK: LOST PROCEDURES

REFERENCE(S):   FAA-H-8083-21, FAA-H-8083-25; AC 61-84; AIM.

Objective.   To determine that the applicant:

1. Exhibits knowledge of the elements related to lost procedures.
2. Selects an appropriate course of action.
3. Maintains an appropriate heading, and climbs, if necessary.
4. Attempts to identify prominent landmark(s).
5. Uses navigation systems/facilities and/or contacts an ATC facility for assistance as appropriate.
6. Plans a precautionary landing if deteriorating weather and/or fuel exhaustion is impending.

VIII. AREA OF OPERATION: EMERGENCY OPERATIONS

NOTE: Tasks F through I are knowledge only TASKs.

A. TASK: POWER FAILURE AT A HOVER

REFERENCE(S): FAA-H-8083-21; POH/RFM.

Objective. To determine that the applicant:

1. Exhibits knowledge of the elements related to power failure at a hover.
2. Determines that the terrain below the aircraft is suitable for a safe touchdown.
3. Performs autorotation from a stationary or forward hover into the wind at recommended altitude, and RPM, while maintaining established heading, ±5°.
4. Touches down with minimum sideward movement, and no rearward movement.
5. Exhibits orientation, division of attention, and proper planning.

B. TASK: POWER FAILURE AT ALTITUDE

NOTE: Simulated power failure at altitude must be given over areas where actual touchdowns can safely be completed in the event of an actual powerplant failure.

REFERENCE(S): FAA-H-8083-21; POH/RFM.

Objective. To determine that the applicant:

1. Exhibits knowledge of the elements related to power failure at altitude.
2. Establishes an autorotation and selects a suitable landing area.
3. Establishes proper aircraft trim and autorotation airspeed, ±5 knots.
4. Maintains rotor RPM within normal limits.
5. Compensates for windspeed and direction as necessary to avoid undershooting or overshooting the selected landing area.
6. Terminates approach with a power recovery at a safe altitude when directed by the examiner.

C. TASK: SYSTEMS AND EQUIPMENT MALFUNCTIONS

REFERENCE(S): FAA-H-8083-21; POH/RFM.

Objective. To determine that the applicant:

1. Exhibits knowledge of the elements related to causes, indications, and pilot actions for various systems and equipment malfunctions.
2. Analyzes the situation and takes action, appropriate to the helicopter used for the practical test, in at least four of the following areas—

    a. engine/oil and fuel.
    b. hydraulic, if applicable.
    c. electrical.
    d. carburetor or induction icing.
    e. smoke and/or fire.
    f. flight control/trim.
    g. pitot static/vacuum and associated flight instruments, if applicable.
    h. rotor and/or antitorque.
    i. various frequency vibrations and the possible components that may be affected.
    j. any other emergency unique to the helicopter flown.

D. TASK: SETTLING-WITH-POWER

REFERENCE(S): FAA-H-8083-21; POH/RFM.

Objective. To determine that the applicant:

1. Exhibits knowledge of the elements related to settling-with-power.
2. Selects an altitude that will allow recovery to be completed no less than 1,000 feet AGL or, if applicable, the manufacturer's recommended altitude, whichever is higher.
3. Promptly recognizes and announces the onset of settling-with-power.
4. Utilizes the appropriate recovery procedure.

E. TASK: LOW ROTOR RPM RECOVERY

REFERENCE(S):   FAA-H-8083-21; Appropriate Manufacturer's Safety Notices; POH/RFM.

NOTE: The examiner may test the applicant orally on this TASK if helicopter used for the practical test has a governor that cannot be disabled.

Objective.   To determine that the applicant:

1. Exhibits knowledge of the elements related to low rotor RPM recovery, including the combination of conditions that are likely to lead to this situation.
2. Detects the development of low rotor RPM and initiates prompt corrective action.
3. Utilizes the appropriate recovery procedure.

F. TASK: DYNAMIC ROLLOVER

REFERENCE(S):   FAA-H-8083-21; AC 90-87; POH/RFM.

Objective.   To determine that the applicant:

1. Exhibits knowledge of the elements related to the aerodynamics of dynamic rollover.
2. Understands the interaction between the antitorque thrust, crosswind, slope, CG, cyclic and collective pitch control in contributing to dynamic rollover.
3. Explains preventive flight technique during takeoffs, landings, and slope operations.

G. TASK: GROUND RESONANCE

REFERENCE(S):   FAA-H-8083-21; POH/RFM.

Objective.   To determine that the applicant:

1. Exhibits knowledge of the elements related to a fully articulated rotor system and the aerodynamics of ground resonance.
2. Understands the conditions that contribute to ground resonance.
3. Explains preventive flight technique during takeoffs and landings.

H. TASK: LOW G CONDITIONS

REFERENCE(S): Helicopter Flight Manual.

Objective. To determine that the applicant:

1. Exhibits knowledge of the elements related to low G conditions.
2. Understands and recognizes the situations that contribute to low G conditions.
3. Explains proper recovery procedures.

I. TASK: EMERGENCY EQUIPMENT AND SURVIVAL GEAR

REFERENCE(S): FAA-H-8083-21; POH/RFM.

Objective. To determine that the applicant:

1. Exhibits knowledge of the elements related to emergency equipment and survival gear appropriate to the helicopter environment encountered during flight.
2. Identifies appropriate equipment that should be on board the helicopter.

FAA-S-8081-16A

IX. AREA OF OPERATION: SPECIAL OPERATIONS

A. TASK: CONFINED AREA OPERATION

REFERENCE(S):   FAA-H-8083-21; POH/RFM.

Objective.   To determine that the applicant:

1. Exhibits knowledge of the elements related to confined area operations.
2. Accomplishes a proper high and low reconnaissance.
3. Selects a suitable approach path, termination point, and departure path.
4. Tracks the selected approach path at an acceptable approach angle and rate of closure to the termination point.
5. Maintains RPM within normal limits.
6. Avoids situations that can result in settling-with-power.
7. Terminates at a hover or on the surface, as conditions allow.
8. Accomplishes a proper ground reconnaissance.
9. Selects a suitable takeoff point, considers factors affecting takeoff and climb performance under various conditions.

B. TASK: PINNACLE/PLATFORM OPERATIONS

REFERENCE(S):   FAA-H-8083-21; POH/RFM.

Objective.   To determine that the applicant:

1. Exhibits knowledge of the elements related to pinnacle/platform operations.
2. Accomplishes a proper high and low reconnaissance.
3. Selects a suitable approach path, termination point, and departure path.
4. Tracks the selected approach path at an acceptable approach angle and rate of closure to the termination point.
5. Maintains RPM within normal limits.
6. Terminates at a hover or on the surface, as conditions allow.
7. Accomplishes a proper ground reconnaissance.
8. Selects a suitable takeoff point, considers factors affecting takeoff and climb performance under various conditions.

X. AREA OF OPERATION: POST-FLIGHT PROCEDURES

A. TASK: AFTER LANDING AND SECURING

REFERENCE(S): FAA-H-8083-21; POH/RFM.

Objective. To determine that the applicant:

1. Exhibits knowledge of the elements related to after-landing, parking, and securing.
2. Minimizes the hazardous effects of rotor downwash during hovering.
3. Parks in an appropriate area, considering the safety of nearby persons and property.
4. Follows the appropriate procedure for engine shutdown.
5. Completes the appropriate checklist.
6. Conducts an appropriate postflight inspection and secures the aircraft.

APPENDIX 1

TASK VS. SIMULATION DEVICE CREDIT

Appendix 1

TASK VS. SIMULATION DEVICE CREDIT

Examiners conducting the Commercial Pilot—Helicopter Practical Tests with simulation devices should consult appropriate documentation to ensure that the device has been approved for training. The documentation for each device should reflect that the following activities have occurred:

1. The device must be evaluated, determined to meet the appropriate standards, and assigned the appropriate qualification level by the National Simulator Program Manager. The device must continue to meet qualification standards through continuing evaluations as outlined in the appropriate advisory circular (AC). For helicopter simulators, AC 120-63 (as amended). Helicopter Simulator Qualification, will be used.

2. The FAA must approve the device for specific TASKs.

3. The device must continue to support the level of student or applicant performance required by this PTS.

NOTE: Users of the following chart are cautioned that use of the chart alone is incomplete. The description and objective of each TASK as listed in the body of the PTS, including all NOTES must also be incorporated for accurate simulation device use.

USE OF CHART

X Creditable.

X1 Creditable only if accomplished in conjunction with a running takeoff or running landing, as appropriate.

NOTE: 1. The helicopter may be used for all TASKs.
2. Level C simulators may be used as indicated only if the applicant meets established pre-requisite experience requirements.
3. Level A helicopter simulator standards have not been defined.
4. Helicopter flight training devices have not been defined.

FLIGHT TASK
Areas of Operation :

FLIGHT SIMULATION DEVICE LEVEL

	1	2	3	4	5	6	7	A	B	C	D
II. Preflight Procedures											
A. Preflight Inspection (Cockpit Only)											
B. Cockpit Management											
C. Engine Starting and Rotor Engagement (If applicable)											
D. Before Takeoff Check											
III. Airport and Heliport Operations											
A. Radio Communications and ATC Light Signals											
B. Traffic Patterns											
C. Airport/Heliport Runway, Heliport, and Taxiway Signs, Markings, and Lighting											
IV. Hovering Maneuvers											
A. Vertical Takeoff and Landing											
B. Slope Operations											
C. Surface Taxi											
D. Hover Taxi											
E. Air Taxi											
V. Takeoffs, Landings, and Go-Arounds											
A. Normal and Crosswind Takeoff and Climb											
B. Normal and Crosswind Approach											
C. Maximum Performance Takeoff and Climb											
D. Steep Approach											
E. Rolling Takeoff											
F. Shallow Approach and Running /Roll-On											
G. Go-Around											

FAA-S-8081-16A

FLIGHT TASK

Areas of Operation:	FLIGHT SIMULATION DEVICE LEVEL										
	1	2	3	4	5	6	7	A	B	C	D
VI. Performance Maneuvers											
A. Rapid Deceleration											
B. Straight In Autorotation											
C. 180° Autorotations											
D. Approach and Landing with Simulated Powerplant Failure – Multiengine Helicopter	—	—	—	—	—	—	—	—	—	—	—
VII. Navigation											
A. Pilotage and Dead Reckoning	—	—	—	—	—	—	—	—	—	X	X
B. Radio Navigation and Radar Services	—	—	—	—	—	—	—	—	—	X	X
C. Diversion	—	—	—	—	—	—	—	—	—	X	X
D. Lost Procedures	—	—	—	—	—	—	—	—	—	X	X
VIII. Emergency Operations											
A. Power Failure at a Hover	—	—	—	—	—	—	—	—	—	X	X
B. Power Failure at Altitude	—	—	—	—	—	—	—	—	—	X	X
C. Systems and Equipment Malfunctions	—	—	—	—	—	—	—	—	—	X	X
D. Settling-With-Power	—	—	—	—	—	—	—	—	—	X	X
E. Low Rotor RPM Recovery	—	—	—	—	—	—	—	—	—	X	X
F. Dynamic Roll Over											
G. Ground Resonance											
H. Low G Conditions	—	—	—	—	—	—	—	—	—	—	—
I. Emergency Equipment and Survival Gear	—	—	—	—	—	—	—	—	—	—	—

FAA-S-8081-16A

U.S. Department
of Transportation

**Federal Aviation
Administration**

FLIGHT INSTRUCTOR

Practical Test Standards

for

ROTORCRAFT

• *HELICOPTER*

December 2006

FLIGHT STANDARDS SERVICE
Washington, DC 20591

NOTE

FAA-S-8081-7B, Flight Instructor - Rotorcraft (Helicopter) Practical Test Standards, will be effective December 1, 2006. All previous editions of this book will be obsolete as of this date.

FOREWORD

The Flight Instructor - Rotorcraft (Helicopter) Practical Test Standards (PTS) book has been published by the Federal Aviation Administration (FAA) to establish the standards for flight instructor certification practical tests for the rotorcraft category, helicopter classes. FAA inspectors and designated pilot examiners shall conduct practical tests in compliance with these standards. Flight instructors and applicants should find these standards helpful during training and when preparing for the practical test.

Joseph K. Tintera, Manager
Regulatory Support Division
Flight Standards Service

CONTENTS

SECTION 1: FLIGHT INSTRUCTOR ROTORCRAFT — HELICOPTER

AREAS OF OPERATION:

INTRODUCTION

The Flight Standards Service of the Federal Aviation Administration (FAA) has developed this practical test book as a standard to be used by FAA inspectors and designated pilot examiners when conducting flight instructor—rotorcraft (helicopter) and flight instructor—rotorcraft (gyroplane) practical tests. Flight instructors are expected to use this book when preparing flight instructor applicants for practical tests. Applicants should be familiar with this book and refer to these standards during their training.

The FAA gratefully acknowledges the valuable assistance provided by many industry participants who contributed their time and talent in assisting with the revision of these practical test standards.

This practical test standard (PTS) book may be purchased from the Superintendent of Documents, U.S. Government Printing Office (GPO), Washington, DC 20402-9325, or from GPO's web site.

http://bookstore.gpo.gov

This PTS is also available for download, in pdf format, from the Flight Standards Service web site.

www.faa.gov

This PTS is published by the U.S. Department of Transportation, Federal Aviation Administration, Airman Testing Standards Branch, AFS-630, P.O. Box 25082, Oklahoma City, OK 73125. Comments regarding this book should be sent, in email form, to the following address.

AFS630comments@faa.gov

Practical Test Standard Concept

Title 14 of the Code of Federal Regulations (14 CFR) specifies the areas in which knowledge and skill shall be demonstrated by an applicant before the issuance of a flight instructor certificate with the associated category and class ratings. The CFRs provide the flexibility that permits the FAA to publish practical test standards containing specific TASKs in which competency shall be demonstrated. The FAA shall revise this book whenever it is determined that changes are needed in the interest of safety. Adherence to provisions of regulations and the practical test standards is mandatory for evaluation of flight instructor applicants.

Flight Instructor Practical Test Book Description

This test book contains the practical test standards for Flight Instructor - Rotorcraft (Helicopter and Gyroplane). Other flight instructor practical test books include:

FAA-S-8081-6, Flight Instructor—Airplane (Single-Engine and Multiengine)
FAA-S-8081-8, Flight Instructor—Glider
FAA-S-8081-9, Flight Instructor—Instrument (Airplane and Helicopter)
FAA-S-8081-11, Flight Instructor—Lighter-Than-Air (Balloon and Airship)

The Flight Instructor Practical Test Standards include the AREAS OF OPERATION and TASKs for the issuance of an initial flight instructor certificate and for the addition of category and/or class ratings to that certificate.

Initial Flight Instructor Certification

An applicant who seeks initial flight instructor certification shall be evaluated in all AREAS OF OPERATION of the standard appropriate to the rating(s) sought. The evaluation shall include at least one TASK in each AREA OF OPERATION and shall always include the required TASKs.

Addition of Aircraft Category and/or Class Ratings to a Flight Instructor Certificate

An applicant who holds a flight instructor certificate and seeks an additional aircraft category and/or class rating shall be evaluated in at least the AREAS OF OPERATION and TASKs that are unique and appropriate to the rating(s) sought (see table at the beginning of each standard). At the discretion of the examiner, an applicant's competence in **all** AREAS OF OPERATION may be evaluated.

Flight Instructor Practical Test Standard Description

AREAS OF OPERATION are phases of the practical test arranged in a logical sequence within each standard. TASKs are knowledge areas, flight procedures, or maneuvers appropriate to an AREA OF OPERATION. In this practical test book, the first AREA OF OPERATION is Fundamentals of Instructing; the last is Postflight Procedures. The examiner may conduct the practical test in any sequence that results in a complete and efficient test; however, **the ground portion of the practical test must be completed prior to the flight portion**.

TASKs are titles of knowledge areas, flight procedures, or maneuvers appropriate to an area of operation.

NOTE is used to emphasis special considerations required in the AREA OF OPERATION or TASK.

REFERENCE identifies the publication(s) that describes the TASK. Descriptions of TASKs and maneuver tolerances are not included in the flight instructor standards because this information can be found in the REFERENCES listed for each TASK. Publications other than those listed may be used as references if their content conveys substantially the same meaning as the referenced publication. REFERENCES listed in this book include current revisions of the following publications:

CFR part 1	Definitions and Abbreviations
CFR part 43	Maintenance, Preventative Maintenance, Rebuilding, and Alteration
CFR part 61	Certification: Pilots and Flight Instructors
CFR part 67	Medical Standards and Certification
CFR part 91	General Operating and Flight Rules
NTSB part 830	Notification and Reporting of Aircraft Accidents and Incidents
FAA-H-8083-1	Aircraft Weight and Balance Handbook
FAA-H-8083-3	Airplane Flying Handbook
FAA-H-8083-9	Aviation Instructor's Handbook
FAA-H-8083-21	Rotorcraft Flying Handbook
FAA-H-8083-25	Pilot's Handbook of Aeronautical Knowledge
AC 00-2	Advisory Circular Checklist
AC 00-6	Aviation Weather
AC 00-45	Aviation Weather Services
AC 60-22	Aeronautical Decision Making
AC 60-28	English Language Requirements Required by 14 CFR parts 61, 63, and 65
AC 61-65	Certification: Pilots and Flight Instructors
AC 61-67	Stall and Spin Awareness Training
AC 61-84	Role of Preflight Preparation
AC 61-98	Currency and Additional Qualification Requirements for Certificated Pilots
AC 61-115	Positive Exchange of Flight Controls Program

AC 61-134	General Aviation Controlled Flight Into Terrain
AC 90-42	Traffic Advisory Practices at Airports Without Operating Control Towers
AC 90-48	Pilots' Role in Collision Avoidance
AC 90-87	Helicopter Dynamic Rollover
AC 91-13	Cold Weather Operation of Aircraft
AC 91-32	Safety In and Around Helicopters
AC 91-42	Hazards of Rotating Propeller and Helicopter Rotor Blades
AC 91-55	Reduction of Electrical System Failure Following Aircraft Engine Starting
FAA-S-8081-15	Private Pilot Practical Test Standards for Rotorcraft
FAA-S-8081-16	Commercial Pilot Practical Test Standards for Rotorcraft
FAA/ASY-20 95/001	Airport Markings, Signs, and Selected Surface Lighting
AIM	Aeronautical Information Manual
POH/AFM	Pilot Operating Handbook and FAA Approved Airplane/Rotorcraft Flight Manual

Each TASK has an Objective. The examiner determines that the applicant meets the TASK Objective through the demonstration of competency in various elements of knowledge and/or skill. The Objectives of TASKs in certain AREAS OF OPERATION, such as Fundamentals of Instructing and Technical Subject Areas, include **only** knowledge elements. The Objectives of TASKs in the AREAS OF OPERATION that include elements of skill as well as knowledge also include common errors which the applicant shall be able to describe, recognize, analyze, and correct.

The Objective of a TASK that involves pilot skill consists of four parts. Those four parts include determination that the applicant exhibits:

1. instructional knowledge of the elements of a TASK. This is accomplished through descriptions, explanations, and simulated instruction;
2. instructional knowledge of common errors related to a TASK, including their recognition, analysis, and correction;
3. the ability to demonstrate and simultaneously explain the key elements of a TASK. The TASK demonstration must be to the COMMERCIAL PILOT skill level; the teaching techniques and procedures should conform to those set forth in FAA-H-8083-9, Aviation Instructor's Handbook, FAA-H-8083-3, Airplane Flying Handbook, and FAA-H-8083-21, Rotorcraft Flying Handbook; and
4. the ability to analyze and correct common errors related to a TASK.

Abbreviations

14 CFR	Title 14 of the Code of Federal Regulations
ADM	Aeronautical Decision Making
AIM	Airman's Information Manual
AIRMETS	Airman's Meteorological Information
ATC	Air Traffic Control
CFIT	Controlled Flight into Terrain
CRM	Crew Resource Management
FAA	Federal Aviation Administration
FDC	Flight Data Center
FSDO	Flight Standards District Office
GPO	Government Printing Office
GPS	Global Positioning System
LAHSO	Land and Hold Short Operations
MEL	Minimum Equipment List
NOTAM	Notice to Airmen
NWS	National Weather Service
PIREPS	Pilot Weather Reports
PTS	Practical Test Standard
SIGMETS	Significant Meteorological Information
SRM	Single Pilot Resource Management
SUA	Special Use Airspace
TFR(s)	Temporary Flight Restriction(s)
VFR	Visual Flight Rules`

Special Emphasis Areas

Examiners shall place special emphasis upon areas of aircraft operation considered critical to flight safety. Among these are:

1. positive aircraft control;
2. positive exchange of the flight controls procedure (who is flying the aircraft);
3. airport operations/runway incursions;
4. collision avoidance;
5. wake turbulence avoidance;
6. land and hold short operations (LAHSO);
7. controlled flight into terrain (CFIT);
8. aeronautical decision making (ADM) and risk management;
9. wire strike avoidance;
10. checklist usage;
11. temporary flight restrictions (TFR);
12. special use airspace (SUA);
13. aviation security; and
14. other areas deemed appropriate to any phase of the practical test.

Although these areas may not be specifically addressed under each TASK, they are essential to flight safety and will be evaluated during the practical test. In all instances, the applicant's actions will relate to the complete situation.

Use of the Practical Test Standards Book

The FAA requires that all practical tests be conducted in accordance with the appropriate Flight Instructor Practical Test Standard and the policies set forth in the INTRODUCTION.

All of the procedures and maneuvers in the Private Pilot and Commercial Pilot Practical Test Standards have been included in the Flight Instructor Practical Test Standards. However, to permit completion of the practical test for initial certification within a reasonable timeframe, the examiner shall select one or more TASKs in each AREA OF OPERATION. In certain AREAS OF OPERATION, there are **required** TASKs which the examiner must select. These required TASKs are identified by a **NOTE** immediately following each AREA OF OPERATION title.

In preparation for the practical test, the examiner shall develop a written "plan of action." The examiner will vary each "plan of action" to ensure that all TASKs in the appropriate practical test standard are evaluated during a given number of practical tests. Except for required TASKs, the examiner should avoid using the same optional TASKs in order to avoid becoming stereotyped. The "plan of action" for a practical test for initial certification shall include one or more TASKs in each AREA OF OPERATION and shall **always** include the required TASKs. The "plan of action" for a practical test for the addition of an aircraft category and/or class rating to a flight instructor certificate shall include the required AREAS OF OPERATION as indicated in the table at the beginning of each standard. The required TASKs appropriate to the additional rating(s) sought shall be included. Any TASK selected for evaluation during the practical test shall be evaluated in its entirety.

The flight instructor applicant shall be prepared in **all** knowledge and skill areas and demonstrate the ability to instruct effectively in **all** TASKs included in the AREAS OF OPERATION of the appropriate practical test standard. Throughout the flight portion of the practical test, the examiner shall evaluate the applicant's ability to demonstrate and simultaneously explain the selected procedures and maneuvers, and to give flight instruction to students at various stages of flight training and levels of experience.

The term "instructional knowledge" means the "what," "why," and "how" of a subject matter topic, procedure, or maneuver. It also means that the flight instructor applicant's discussions, explanations, and descriptions should follow the recommended teaching procedures and techniques explained in FAA-H-8083-9, Aviation Instructor's Handbook.

The purpose for including common errors in certain TASKs is to assist the examiner in determining that the flight instructor applicant has the ability to recognize, analyze, and correct such errors. **The examiner shall not simulate any condition that may jeopardize safe flight or result in possible damage to the aircraft.** The common errors listed in the TASK Objectives may or may not be found in the TASK References. However, the FAA considers their frequency of occurrence justification for their inclusion in the TASK Objectives.

The examiner shall place special emphasis on the applicant's demonstrated ability to teach precise aircraft control and sound judgment in decision making. Evaluation of the applicant's ability to teach judgment shall be accomplished by asking the applicant to describe the oral discussions and the presentation of practical problems that would be used in instructing students in the exercise of sound judgment. The examiner shall also emphasize the evaluation of the applicant's demonstrated ability to teach spatial disorientation, wake turbulence, and low level wind shear avoidance, checklist usage, positive exchange of flight controls, and any other directed special emphasis areas.

Flight Instructor Practical Test Prerequisites

An applicant for a flight instructor **initial** certification practical test is required by the CFRs to:

1. have reached the age of 18 years;
2. read, speak, write, and understand the English language;
3. hold a commercial pilot or airline transport pilot certificate with an aircraft rating appropriate to the flight instructor rating sought;
4. hold an instrument rating in the category and class in which the instrument instructor privileges are being sought;
5. have passed the appropriate flight instructor knowledge test(s) since the beginning of the 24th month before the month in which he or she takes the practical test;
6. have the prescribed aeronautical experience and instruction for a flight instructor certificate with the rating sought; and
7. obtain a written statement from an appropriately certificated and qualified flight instructor certifying that the applicant has been given flight instruction in the AREAS OF OPERATION listed in 14 CFR part 61, section 61.187 for the flight instructor rating sought in preparation for the practical test within 60 days preceding the date of application. The statement shall also state that the instructor finds the applicant competent to pass the practical test, and that the applicant has satisfactory knowledge of the subject area(s) in which a deficiency was indicated on the knowledge test report.[1]

---

[1]AC 61-65, Certification: Pilots and Flight Instructors, states that the instructor may sign the recommendation on the reverse side of FAA Form 8710-1, Airman Certificate and/or Rating Application, in lieu of this statement, provided all appropriate 14 CFR part 61 requirements are substantiated by reliable records.

An applicant holding a flight instructor certificate who applies for an **additional** rating on that certificate is required by the CFRs to:

1. hold an effective pilot certificate with ratings appropriate to the flight instructor rating sought;
2. have at least 15 hours as pilot in command in the category and class aircraft appropriate to the rating sought;
3. have passed the appropriate knowledge test prescribed for the issuance of a flight instructor certificate with the rating sought since the beginning of the 24th month before the month in which he or she takes the practical test; and
4. obtain a written statement from an appropriately certificated and qualified flight instructor certifying that the applicant has been given flight instruction in the applicable AREAS OF OPERATION listed in 14 CFR part 61, section 61.187 for the flight instructor rating sought in preparation for the practical test within 60 days preceding the date of application. The statement shall also state that the instructor finds the applicant competent to pass the practical test, and that the applicant has satisfactory knowledge of the subject area(s) in which a deficiency was indicated on the knowledge test report.[1] Although 14 CFR part 61, section 61.191 refers to additional flight instructor ratings, the basis for the knowledge and practical tests required for any additional flight instructor rating can be found in 14 CFR part 61, section 61.187(a).

Aircraft and Equipment Required for the Practical Test

The flight instructor applicant is required by 14 CFR part 61, section 61.45 to provide an airworthy, certificated aircraft for use during the practical test. This section further requires that the aircraft:

1. have fully functioning dual controls except as provided in 14 CFR part 61, section 61.45; and
2. be capable of performing **all** appropriate TASKs for the flight instructor rating sought and have no operating limitations that would prohibit the performance of any TASK. (**NOTE:** A touchdown autorotation is a required TASK for the flight instructor - helicopter practical test.)

Use of Simulators and Flight Training Devices

All flight instructor practical tests shall be conducted in accordance with 14 CFR part 61, section 61.45 and in an actual aircraft. Use of an approved simulator or flight training device (FTD) is not authorized for any in-flight TASK of a flight instructor practical test unless approved in the practical test standards or under conditions and limitations of a regulatory exemption. However, such devices may be used to assist in evaluating the instructional ability of an applicant during any TASK not involving a flight maneuver.

Flight Instructor Responsibility

An appropriately rated flight instructor is responsible for training the flight instructor applicant to acceptable standards in **all** subject matter areas, procedures, and maneuvers included in the TASKs within each AREA OF OPERATION in the appropriate flight instructor practical test standard. Flight instructors shall use a written training syllabus containing, as a minimum, every TASK in the practical test standard when training applicants. This will not only ensure coverage of all TASKs that may be evaluated during a practical test but also satisfy the requirement for maintaining a copy of the training syllabus used to train each applicant.

Because of the impact of their teaching activities in developing safe, proficient pilots, flight instructors should exhibit a high level of knowledge, skill, and the ability to impart that knowledge and skill to students. The flight instructor shall certify that the applicant is:

1. able to make a practical application of the fundamentals of instructing;
2. competent to teach the subject matter, procedures, and maneuvers included in the standards to students with varying backgrounds and levels of experience and ability;
3. able to perform the procedures and maneuvers included in the standards to at least the COMMERCIAL PILOT skill level[2] while giving effective flight instruction; and
4. competent to pass the required practical test for the issuance of the flight instructor certificate with the associated category and class ratings or the addition of a category and/or class rating to a flight instructor certificate.

Throughout the applicant's training, the flight instructor is responsible for emphasizing the performance of, and the ability to teach, effective visual scanning and collision avoidance procedures.

Positive Exchange of Flight Controls

During flight training, there must always be a clear understanding between students and flight instructors of who has control of the aircraft. Prior to flight, a briefing should be conducted that includes the procedure for the exchange of flight controls. A positive three-step process in the exchange of flight controls between pilots is a proven procedure and one that is strongly recommended.

---

[2]Commercial Pilot skill level is defined as performing a procedure or maneuver within the tolerances listed in the FAA Commercial Pilot Practical Test Standards. If the maneuver appears only in the Private Pilot Practical Test Standards, the term means that the applicant's performance is expected to be more precise than indicated by the stated tolerances.

When the instructor wishes the student to take control of the aircraft, he/she will say "You have the flight controls." The student acknowledges immediately by saying, "I have the flight controls." The flight instructor again says "You have the flight controls." When control is returned to the instructor, follow the same procedure. A visual check is recommended to verify that the exchange has occurred. There should never be any doubt as to who is flying the aircraft.

Examiner[3] Responsibility

The examiner who conducts the practical test is responsible for determining that the applicant meets acceptable standards of teaching ability, knowledge, and skill in the selected TASKs. The examiner makes this determination by accomplishing an Objective that is appropriate to each selected TASK, and includes an evaluation of the applicant's:

1. ability to apply the fundamentals of instructing;
2. knowledge of, and ability to teach, the subject matter, procedures, and maneuvers covered in the TASKs;
3. ability to perform the procedures and maneuvers included in the standards to at least the COMMERCIAL PILOT skill level while giving effective flight instruction; and
4. ability to analyze and correct common errors related to the procedures and maneuvers covered in the TASKs.

It is intended that oral questioning be used at any time during the practical test to determine that the applicant can instruct effectively and has a comprehensive knowledge of the TASKs and their related safety factors.

During the flight portion of the practical test, the examiner shall act as a student during selected maneuvers. This will give the examiner an opportunity to evaluate the flight instructor applicant's ability to analyze and correct simulated common errors related to these maneuvers.

Satisfactory Performance

The practical test is passed if, in the judgment of the examiner, the applicant demonstrates satisfactory performance with regard to:

1. knowledge of the fundamentals of instructing;
2. knowledge of the technical subject areas;
3. knowledge of the flight instructor's responsibilities concerning the pilot certification process;
4. knowledge of the flight instructor's responsibilities concerning logbook entries and pilot certificate endorsements;
5. ability to demonstrate the procedures and maneuvers selected by the examiner to at least the COMMERCIAL PILOT skill level while giving effective instruction;

---

[3]The word "examiner" is used throughout the standards to denote either the FAA inspector or FAA designated pilot examiner or other authorized person who conducts an official practical test.

6. competence in teaching the procedures and maneuvers selected by the examiner;
7. competence in describing, recognizing, analyzing, and correcting common errors simulated by the examiner; and
8. knowledge of the development and effective use of a course of training, a syllabus, and a lesson plan.

Unsatisfactory Performance

If, in the judgment of the examiner, the applicant does not meet the standards of performance of any TASK performed, the associated AREA OF OPERATION is considered unsatisfactory and, therefore, the practical test is failed. The examiner or applicant may discontinue the test at any time when the failure of an AREA OF OPERATION makes the applicant ineligible for the certificate or rating sought. The test may be continued only with the consent of the applicant. If the test is discontinued, the applicant is entitled to credit for only those AREAS OF OPERATION satisfactorily performed. However, during the retest and at the discretion of the examiner, any TASK may be re-evaluated including those previously considered satisfactory. Specific reasons for disqualification are:

1. failure to perform a procedure or maneuver to the COMMERCIAL PILOT skill level while giving effective flight instruction;
2. failure to provide an effective instructional explanation while demonstrating a procedure or maneuver (explanation during the demonstration must be clear, concise, technically accurate, and complete with no prompting from the examiner);
3. any action or lack of action by the applicant which requires corrective intervention by the examiner to maintain safe flight;
4. failure to use proper and effective visual scanning techniques to clear the area before and while performing maneuvers.

When a notice of disapproval is issued, the examiner will record the applicant's unsatisfactory performance in terms of AREAS OF OPERATION and TASKs.

Letter of Discontinuance

When a practical test is discontinued for reasons other than unsatisfactory performance (i.e., equipment failure, weather, or illness) FAA Form 8700-1, Airman Certificate and/or Rating Application, and, if applicable, the Airman Knowledge Test Report, shall be returned to the applicant. The examiner at that time shall prepare, sign, and issue a Letter of Discontinuance to the applicant. The Letter of Discontinuance should identify the AREAS OF OPERATION and their associated TASKs of the practical test that were successfully completed. The applicant shall be advised that the Letter of Discontinuance shall be presented to the examiner when the practical test is resumed, and made part of the certification file.

Aeronautical Decision Making and Risk Management

The examiner shall evaluate the applicant's ability throughout the practical test to use good aeronautical decision making procedures in order to evaluate risks. The examiner shall accomplish this requirement by developing scenarios that incorporate as many TASKs as possible to evaluate the applicants risk management in making safe aeronautical decisions. For example, the examiner may develop a scenario that incorporates weather decisions and performance planning.

The applicant's ability to utilize all the assets available in making a risk analysis to determine the safest course of action is essential for satisfactory performance. The scenarios should be realistic and within the capabilities of the aircraft used for the practical test.

Single-Pilot Resource Management

Single-Pilot Resource Management refers to the effective use of ALL available resources: human resources, hardware, and information. It is similar to Crew Resource Management (CRM) procedures that are being emphasized in multi-crewmember operations except that only one crewmember (the pilot) is involved. Human resources "...includes all other groups routinely working with the pilot who are involved in decisions that are required to operate a flight safely. These groups include, but are not limited to: dispatchers, weather briefers, maintenance personnel, and air traffic controllers." Single-pilot Resource Management; is a set of skill competencies that must be evident in all TASKs in this practical test standard as applied to single-pilot operation.

SECTION 1

FLIGHT INSTRUCTOR ROTORCRAFT - HELICOPTER

Practical Test Standards

FAA-S-8081-7B

CONTENTS: SECTION 1

X. PERFORMANCE MANEUVERS

XI. EMERGENCY OPERATIONS

XII. SPECIAL OPERATIONS

XIII. POSTFLIGHT PROCEDURES

ADDITIONAL RATING TABLE

ADDITION OF A HELICOPTER CLASS RATING (AND A ROTORCRAFT CATEGORY RATING, IF APPROPRIATE) TO A FLIGHT INSTRUCTOR CERTIFICATE

REQUIRED AREAS OF OPERATION	FLIGHT INSTRUCTOR CERTIFICATE AND RATING HELD					
	ASE	AME	RG	G	IA	IH
I	N	N	N	N	N	N
II	Y	Y	Y	Y	Y	Y
III	Y	Y	Y	Y	Y	Y
IV	N	N	N	N	N	N
V	Y	Y	Y	Y	Y	Y
VI	N	N	N	N	N	N
VII	Y	Y	Y	Y	Y	Y
VIII	Y	Y	Y	Y	Y	Y
IX	Y	Y	Y	Y	Y	Y
X	Y	Y	Y	Y	Y	Y
XI	Y	Y	Y	Y	Y	Y
XII	Y	Y	Y	Y	Y	Y
XIII	Y	Y	Y	Y	Y	Y

LEGEND

ASE   Airplane Single-Engine
AME   Airplane Multiengine
RG   Rotorcraft Gyroplane
G   Glider Powered
IA   Instrument Airplane/Helicopter
IH   Instrument Helicopter

NOTE: If an applicant holds more than one rating on a flight instructor certificate and the table indicates both a Y (Yes) and an N (No) for a particular AREA OF OPERATION, the N entry applies. This is logical since the applicant has satisfactorily accomplished the AREA OF OPERATION on a previous flight instructor practical test. At the discretion of the examiner, the applicant's competence in all AREAS OF OPERATION may be evaluated.

RENEWAL OR REINSTATEMENT
OF A FLIGHT INSTRUCTOR

REQUIRED AREAS OF OPERATION	NUMBER OF TASKS
II	TASK L and 1 other TASK
III	1
IV	1
V	1
VI	1
VII	1
VIII	2 Takeoffs and 2 Landings
IX	1

The renewal or reinstatement of one rating on a Flight Instructor Certificate renews or reinstates all privileges existing on the certificate. (14 CFR part 61, sections 61.197 and 61.199)

FAA-S-8081-7B

APPLICANT'S PRACTICAL TEST CHECKLIST
(HELICOPTER)

APPOINTMENT WITH EXAMINER:

EXAMINER'S NAME_____

LOCATION _____

DATE/TIME _____

ACCEPTABLE AIRCRAFT

☐ Aircraft Documents:
     Airworthiness Certificate
     Registration Certificate
     Operating Limitations
☐ Aircraft Maintenance Records:
     Logbook Record of Airworthiness Inspections and AD Compliance

PERSONAL EQUIPMENT

☐ Practical Test Standard
☐ Lesson Plan Library
☐ Current Aeronautical Charts
☐ Computer and Plotter
☐ Flight Plan and Flight Log Forms
☐ Current AIM, Airport Facility Directory, and Appropriate Publications

PERSONAL RECORDS

☐ Identification—Photo/Signature ID
☐ Pilot Certificate
☐ Current and Appropriate Medical Certificate
☐ Completed FAA Form 8710-1, Airman Certificate
     and/or Rating Application
☐ AC Form 8080-2, Airman Written Test Report or Computer
     Test Report
☐ Pilot Logbook with Appropriate Instructor Endorsements
☐ FAA Form 8060-5, Notice of Disapproval (if applicable)
☐ Approved School Graduation Certificate (if applicable)
☐ Examiner's Fee (if applicable)

EXAMINER'S PRACTICAL TEST CHECKLIST
FLIGHT INSTRUCTOR - ROTORCRAFT
(HELICOPTER)

APPLICANT'S NAME _____

LOCATION _____

DATE/TIME _____

I. FUNDAMENTALS OF INSTRUCTING

- ☐ **A.** The Learning Process
- ☐ **B.** Human Behavior
- ☐ **C.** The Teaching Process
- ☐ **D.** Teaching Methods
- ☐ **E.** Critique and Evaluation
- ☐ **F.** Flight Instructor Characteristics and Responsibilities
- ☐ **G.** Planning Instructional Activity

II. TECHNICAL SUBJECTS

- ☐ **A.** Aeromedical Factors
- ☐ **B.** Visual Scanning and Collision Avoidance
- ☐ **C.** Use of Distractions During Flight Training
- ☐ **D.** Principles of Flight
- ☐ **E.** Helicopter Flight Controls
- ☐ **F.** Helicopter Weight and Balance
- ☐ **G.** Navigation and Flight Planning
- ☐ **H.** Night Operations
- ☐ **I.** Regulations and Publications
- ☐ **J.** Airworthiness Requirements
- ☐ **K.** National Airspace System
- ☐ **L.** Logbook Entries and Certificate Endorsements

III. PREFLIGHT PREPARATION

- ☐ **A.** Certificates and Documents
- ☐ **B.** Weather Information
- ☐ **C.** Operation of Systems
- ☐ **D.** Performance and Limitations

IV. PREFLIGHT LESSON ON A MANEUVER TO BE PERFORMED IN FLIGHT

☐ **A.** Maneuver Lesson

V. PREFLIGHT PROCEDURES

☐ **A.** Preflight Inspection
☐ **B.** Single-Pilot Resource Management
☐ **C.** Engine Starting and Rotor Engagement
☐ **D.** Before Takeoff Check

VI. AIRPORT AND HELIPORT OPERATIONS

☐ **A.** Radio Communications and ATC Light Signals
☐ **B.** Traffic Patterns
☐ **C.** Airport and Heliport Markings and Lighting

VII. HOVERING MANEUVERS

☐ **A.** Vertical Takeoff and Landing
☐ **B.** Surface Taxi
☐ **C.** Hover Taxi
☐ **D.** Air Taxi
☐ **E.** Slope Operation

VIII. TAKEOFFS, LANDINGS, AND GO-AROUNDS

☐ **A.** Normal and Crosswind Takeoff and Climb
☐ **B.** Maximum Performance Takeoff and Climb
☐ **C.** Rolling Takeoff
☐ **D.** Normal and Crosswind Approach
☐ **E.** Steep Approach
☐ **F.** Shallow Approach and Running/Roll-On Landing
☐ **G.** Go-Around
☐ **H.** Approach and Landing with Simulated Powerplant Failure – Multiengine Helicopter

IX. FUNDAMENTALS OF FLIGHT

☐ **A.** Straight-and-Level Flight
☐ **B.** Level Turns
☐ **C.** Straight Climbs and Climbing Turns
☐ **D.** Straight Descents and Descending Turns

X. PERFORMANCE MANEUVERS

- ☐ **A.** Rapid Deceleration
- ☐ **B.** Straight-In Autorotation
- ☐ **C.** 180° Autorotation

XI. EMERGENCY OPERATIONS

- ☐ **A.** Power Failure at a Hover
- ☐ **B.** Power Failure at Altitude
- ☐ **C.** Settling-With-Power
- ☐ **D.** Low Rotor RPM Recovery
- ☐ **E.** Anti-torque System Failure
- ☐ **F.** Dynamic Rollover
- ☐ **G.** Ground Resonance
- ☐ **H.** Low "G" Conditions
- ☐ **I.** Systems and Equipment Malfunctions
- ☐ **J.** Emergency Equipment and Survival Gear

XII. SPECIAL OPERATIONS

- ☐ **A.** Confined Area Operation
- ☐ **B.** Pinnacle/Platform Operation

XIII. POSTFLIGHT PROCEDURES

- ☐ **A.** After-Landing and Securing

FAA-S-8081-7B

I. AREA OF OPERATION: FUNDAMENTALS OF INSTRUCTING

NOTE: The examiner shall select at least TASKs E and F.

A. TASK: THE LEARNING PROCESS

REFERENCE: FAA-H-8083-9.

Objective. To determine that the applicant exhibits instructional knowledge of the elements of the learning process by describing:

1. The definition and characteristics of learning.
2. Practical application of the laws of learning.
3. Factors involved in how people learn.
4. Recognition and proper use of the various levels of learning.
5. Principles that are applied in learning a skill.
6. Factors related to forgetting and retention.
7. How the transfer of learning affects the learning process.
8. How the formation of habit patterns affects the learning process.

B. TASK: HUMAN BEHAVIOR

REFERENCE: FAA-H-8083-9.

Objective. To determine that the applicant exhibits instructional knowledge of the elements related to human behavior by describing:

1. Control of human behavior.
2. Development of student potential.
3. Relationship of human needs to behavior and learning.
4. Relationship of defense mechanisms to student learning and pilot decision making.
5. General rules which a flight instructor should follow during student training to ensure good human relations.

C. TASK: THE TEACHING PROCESS

REFERENCE: FAA-H-8083-9.

Objective. To determine that the applicant exhibits instructional knowledge of the elements of the teaching process by describing:

1. Preparation of a lesson for a ground or flight instructional period.
2. Presentation of knowledge and skills, including the methods, which are suitable in particular situations.
3. Application, by the student, of the knowledge and skills presented by the instructor.
4. Review of the material presented and the evaluation of student performance and accomplishment.

D. TASK: TEACHING METHODS

REFERENCE: FAA-H-8083-9.

Objective. To determine that the applicant exhibits instructional knowledge of the elements of teaching methods by describing:

1. The organization of a lesson, i.e., introduction, development, and conclusion.
2. The lecture method.
3. The guided discussion method.
4. The demonstration-performance method.
5. Computer/video assisted instruction.

E. TASK: CRITIQUE AND EVALUATION

REFERENCE: FAA-H-8083-9.

Objective. To determine that the applicant exhibits instructional knowledge of the elements of critique and evaluation by describing:

1. Purpose and characteristics of an effective critique.
2. Difference between critique and evaluation.
3. Characteristics of effective oral questions and what type to avoid.
4. Responses to student questions.
5. Characteristics and development of effective written tests.
6. Characteristics and uses of performance tests, specifically, the FAA practical test standards.

F. TASK: FLIGHT INSTRUCTOR CHARACTERISTICS AND RESPONSIBILITIES

REFERENCE: FAA-H-8083-9.

Objective. To determine that the applicant exhibits instructional knowledge of the elements of flight instructor characteristics and responsibilities by describing:

1. Major characteristics and qualifications of a professional flight instructor.
2. Role of the flight instructor in dealing with student stress, anxiety, and psychological abnormalities.
3. Flight instructor's responsibility with regard to student pilot supervision and surveillance.
4. Flight instructor's authority and responsibility for endorsements and recommendations.
5. Flight instructor's responsibility in the conduct of the required FAA flight review.

G. TASK: PLANNING INSTRUCTIONAL ACTIVITY

REFERENCE: FAA-H-8083-9.

Objective. To determine that the applicant exhibits instructional knowledge of the elements related to the planning of instructional activity by describing:

1. Development of a course of training.
2. Content and use of a training syllabus.
3. Purpose, characteristics, proper use, and items of a lesson plan.
4. Flexibility features of a course of training, syllabus, and lesson plan required to accommodate students with varying backgrounds, levels of experience, and ability.

II. AREA OF OPERATION: TECHNICAL SUBJECTS

NOTE: The examiner shall select TASK L and at least one other TASK.

A. TASK: AEROMEDICAL FACTORS

REFERENCES: FAA-H-8083-25; AIM.

Objective. To determine that the applicant exhibits instructional knowledge of the elements related to aeromedical factors by describing:

1. Hypoxia, its symptoms, effects, and corrective action.
2. Hyperventilation, its symptoms, effects, and corrective action.
3. Middle ear and sinus problems, their causes, effects, and corrective action.
4. Spatial disorientation, its causes, effects, and corrective action.
5. Motion sickness, its causes, effects, and corrective action.
6. Effects of alcohol and drugs, and their relationship to safety.
7. Carbon monoxide poisoning, its symptoms, effects, and corrective action.
8. How evolved gas from scuba diving can affect a pilot during flight.
9. Fatigue, its effects and corrective action.

B. TASK: VISUAL SCANNING AND COLLISION AVOIDANCE

REFERENCES: FAA-H-8083-25; AC 90-48; AIM.

Objective. To determine that the applicant exhibits instructional knowledge of the elements related to visual scanning and collision avoidance by describing:

1. Relationship between a pilot's physical or mental condition and vision.
2. Environmental conditions and optical illusions that affect vision.
3. "See and avoid" concept.
4. Practice of "time sharing" of attention inside and outside the cockpit.
5. Proper visual scanning technique.
6. Relationship between poor visual scanning habits, aircraft speed differential, and increased collision risk.
7. Appropriate clearing procedures.
8. Situations which involve the greatest collision risk.

C. TASK: USE OF DISTRACTIONS DURING FLIGHT TRAINING

REFERENCE: FAA-H-8083-9.

Objective. To determine that the applicant exhibits instructional knowledge of the elements related to use of distractions during flight training by describing:

1. Flight situations where pilot distraction can be a causal factor related to aircraft accidents.
2. Selection of realistic distractions for specific flight situations.
3. Relationship between division of attention and flight instructor use of distractions.
4. Difference between proper use of distractions and harassment.

D. TASK: PRINCIPLES OF FLIGHT

REFERENCE: FAA-H-8083-21.

Objective. To determine that the applicant exhibits instructional knowledge of the elements related to principles of flight by describing:

1. Characteristics of different rotor systems.
2. Effect of lift, weight, thrust, and drag during various flight maneuvers.
3. Retreating blade stall.
4. Torque effect.
5. Dissymmetry of lift.
6. Blade flapping and coning.
7. Coriolis effect.
8. Translating tendency.
9. Translational lift.
10. Transverse flow effect.
11. Pendular action.

E. TASK: HELICOPTER FLIGHT CONTROLS

REFERENCE: FAA-H-8083-21.

Objective. To determine that the applicant exhibits instructional knowledge of the elements related to flight controls of the helicopter used for the practical test by describing:

1. Collective pitch control.
2. Cyclic pitch control.
3. Anti-torque control.
4. Throttle control.

F. TASK: HELICOPTER WEIGHT AND BALANCE

REFERENCES: FAA-H-8083-1, FAA-H-8083-21.

Objective. To determine that the applicant exhibits instructional knowledge of the elements related to weight and balance by describing:

1. Weight and balance terms.
2. Effect of weight and balance on performance.
3. Determination of total weight, center of gravity (longitudinal and lateral), and changes that occur when adding, removing, or shifting weight.

G. TASK: NAVIGATION AND FLIGHT PLANNING

REFERENCES: FAA-H-8083-25.

Objective. To determine that the applicant exhibits instructional knowledge of the elements related to navigation and flight planning by describing:

1. Terms used in navigation.
2. Features of aeronautical charts.
3. Importance of using proper and current aeronautical charts.
4. Identification of various types of airspace.
5. Method of plotting a course, selection of fuel stops and alternates, and appropriate actions in the event of unforeseen situations.
6. Fundamentals of pilotage and dead reckoning.
7. Fundamentals of radio navigation.
8. Diversion to an alternate.
9. Lost procedures.
10. Computation of fuel requirement.
11. Importance of preparing and properly using a flight log.
12. Importance of a weather check and the use of good judgment in making a "go/no-go" decision.
13. Purpose of, and procedure used in, filing a flight plan.
14. Global positioning system (GPS).

H. TASK: NIGHT OPERATIONS

REFERENCES: FAA-H-8083-21, FAA-H-8083-25; AIM; FAA-S-8081-15.

Objective. To determine that the applicant exhibits instructional knowledge of the elements related to night operations by describing:

1. Factors related to night vision, disorientation, and optical illusions.
2. Weather considerations specific to night operations.
3. Preflight inspection, including windshield and window cleanliness.
4. Proper adjustment of interior lights, including availability of flashlight.
5. Use of position and anticollision lights prior to, during, and after engine start.
6. Hover taxiing and orientation on an airport or heliport.
7. Takeoff and climb-out.
8. Inflight orientation.
9. Importance of verifying the helicopter's attitude by visual references and flight instruments.
10. Recovery from critical flight attitudes by visual references and flight instruments.
11. Emergencies such as electrical failure, engine malfunction, and emergency landings.
12. Traffic patterns.
13. Approaches and landings with and without landing lights.

I. TASK: REGULATIONS AND PUBLICATIONS

REFERENCES: 14 CFR parts 1, 61, 91; NTSB Part 830; AC 00-2; AIM, Rotorcraft Flight Manual.

Objective. To determine that the applicant exhibits instructional knowledge of the elements related to pertinent regulations and publications, their purpose, general content, availability, and method of revision, by describing:

1. 14 CFR parts 1, 61, and 91.
2. NTSB Part 830.
3. Flight information publications.
4. Practical Test Standards.
5. Helicopter Flight Manual (as applicable).

J. TASK: AIRWORTHINESS REQUIREMENTS

REFERENCES: 14 CFR parts 1, 27, 29, 39, 43, and 91; FAA-H-8083-21.

Objective. To determine that the applicant exhibits knowledge of the elements related to airworthiness requirements by:

1. Explaining—

   a. required instruments and equipment for day/night VFR.
   b. procedures and limitations for determining airworthiness of the helicopter with inoperative instruments and equipment with and without an MEL.
   c. requirements and procedures for obtaining a special flight permit.

2. Locating and explaining—

   a. airworthiness directives.
   b. compliance records.
   c. maintenance/inspection requirements.
   d. appropriate record keeping.

K. TASK: NATIONAL AIRSPACE SYSTEM

REFERENCES: 14 CFR part 91; FAA-S-8081-12, FAA-S-8081-14; AIM.

Objective. To determine that the applicant exhibits instructional knowledge of the elements of the national airspace system by describing:

1. Basic VFR Weather Minimums—for all classes of airspace.
2. Airspace classes—the operating rules, pilot certification, and aircraft equipment requirements for the following—

   a. Class A.
   b. Class B.
   c. Class C.
   d. Class D.
   e. Class E.
   f. Class G.

3. Special use airspace and other airspace areas.
4. Temporary flight restrictions (TFRs).

L. TASK: LOGBOOK ENTRIES AND CERTIFICATE ENDORSEMENTS

REFERENCES: 14 CFR part 61; AC 61-65, AC 61-98.

Objective. To determine that the applicant exhibits instructional knowledge of the elements related to logbook entries and certificate endorsements by describing:

1. Required logbook entries for instruction given.
2. Required student pilot certificate endorsements, including appropriate logbook entries.
3. Preparation of a recommendation for a pilot practical test, including appropriate logbook entry.
4. Required endorsement of a pilot logbook for the satisfactory completion of an FAA flight review.
5. Required flight instructor records.

III. AREA OF OPERATION: PREFLIGHT PREPARATION

NOTE: The examiner shall select at least one TASK.

A. TASK: CERTIFICATES AND DOCUMENTS

REFERENCES: 14 CFR parts 43, 61, 67, 91; FAA-H-8083-21, FAA-H-8083-25; Rotorcraft Flight Manual.

Objective. To determine that the applicant exhibits instructional knowledge of the elements related to certificates and documents by describing:

1. Requirements for the issuance of pilot and flight instructor certificates and ratings, and the privileges and limitations of those certificates and ratings.
2. Medical certificates, class, duration, and how to obtain them.
3. Airworthiness and registration certificates.
4. Helicopter handbooks and manuals.
5. Helicopter maintenance requirements and records.

B. TASK: WEATHER INFORMATION

REFERENCES: AC 00-6, AC 00-45, AC 61-84; FAA-H-8083-25; AIM.

Objective. To determine that the applicant exhibits instructional knowledge of the elements related to weather information by describing:

1. Importance of a thorough weather check.
2. Various sources for obtaining weather information.
3. Use of weather reports, forecasts, and charts.
4. Use of PIREPs, SIGMETs, and AIRMETs.
5. Recognition of aviation weather hazards to include wind shear.
6. Factors to be considered in making a "go/no-go" decision.

C. TASK: OPERATION OF SYSTEMS

REFERENCES: FAA-H-8083-21; Rotorcraft Flight Manual.

Objective. To determine that the applicant exhibits instructional knowledge of the elements related to operation of systems, as applicable to the helicopter used for the practical test, by describing:

1. Powerplant, including controls, indicators, cooling, and fire detection.
2. Main rotor system.
3. Anti-torque system.
4. Landing gear, brakes, and steering system.
5. Fuel, oil, and hydraulic systems.
6. Electrical system.
7. Environmental system.
8. Pitot static/vacuum system and associated instruments.
9. Anti-icing systems.
10. Avionics equipment.

D. TASK: PERFORMANCE AND LIMITATIONS

REFERENCES: AC 61-84, FAA-H-8083-1, FAA-H-8083-21; Rotorcraft Flight Manual.

Objective. To determine that the applicant exhibits instructional knowledge of the elements related to performance and limitations by describing:

1. Determination of weight and balance condition.
2. Use of performance charts and other data for determining performance in various phases of flight.
3. Effects of density altitude and other atmospheric conditions on performance.
4. Factors to be considered when operating within "avoid" areas of the height/velocity diagram.
5. Conditions that may cause loss of tail rotor effectiveness/ unanticipated loss of directional control.
6. Other factors to be considered in determining that required performance is within the helicopter's capabilities.

IV. AREA OF OPERATION: PREFLIGHT LESSON ON A MANEUVER TO BE PERFORMED IN FLIGHT

NOTE: Examiner shall select at least one maneuver from AREAS OF OPERATION VII through XII, and ask the applicant to present a preflight lesson on the selected maneuver as the lesson would be taught to a student. Previously developed lesson plans from the applicant's library may be used.

A. TASK: MANEUVER LESSON

REFERENCES: FAA-H-8083-9, FAA-H-8083-21; FAA-S-8081-15, FAA-S-8081-16; Rotorcraft Flight Manual.

Objective. To determine that the applicant exhibits instructional knowledge of the selected maneuver by:

1. Using a lesson plan that includes all essential items to make an effective and organized presentation.
2. Stating the objective.
3. Giving an accurate, comprehensive oral description of the maneuver, including the elements and associated common errors.
4. Using instructional aids, as appropriate.
5. Describing the recognition, analysis, and correction of common errors.

V. AREA OF OPERATION: PREFLIGHT PROCEDURES

NOTE: The examiner shall select at least one TASK.

A. TASK: PREFLIGHT INSPECTION

REFERENCES: FAA-H-8083-9, FAA-H-8083-21; FAA-S-8081-15, FAA-S-8081-16; Rotorcraft Flight Manual.

Objective. To determine that the applicant:

1. Exhibits instructional knowledge of the elements of a preflight inspection, as applicable to the helicopter used for the practical test, by describing—

   a. reasons for the preflight inspection, items that should be inspected, and how defects are detected.
   b. importance of using the appropriate checklist.
   c. removal of control locks, rotor blade tie-down, and wheel chocks, if applicable.
   d. determination of fuel, oil, and hydraulic fluid quantity, possible contamination and/or leaks.
   e. inspection of flight controls.
   f. detection of visible structural damage.
   g. importance of proper loading and securing of baggage and equipment.
   h. use of sound judgment in determining whether the helicopter is in condition for safe flight.

2. Exhibits instructional knowledge of common errors related to a preflight inspection by describing—

   a. failure to use or improper use of checklist.
   b. hazards which may result from allowing distractions to interrupt a preflight inspection.
   c. inability to recognize discrepancies.
   d. failure to ensure servicing with the proper fuel and oil.

3. Demonstrates and simultaneously explains a preflight inspection from an instructional standpoint.

FAA-S-8081-7B

B. TASK: SINGLE-PILOT RESOURCE MANAGEMENT

REFERENCES: FAA-H-8083-9, AC 91-32; CFR part 91; FAA-S-8081-15, FAA-S-8081-16; Rotorcraft Flight Manual.

Objective. To determine that the applicant:

1. Exhibits instructional knowledge of the elements of crew resource management by describing—

    a. proper arranging and securing of essential materials and equipment in the cockpit.
    b. proper use and/or adjustment of such cockpit items as safety belts, shoulder harnesses, anti-torque pedals, and seats.
    c. occupant briefing on emergency procedures, rotor blade avoidance, and use of safety belts and shoulder harnesses.
    d. utilization of all available human resources, maintenance personnel, weather briefers, and air traffic control, and other groups routinely working with the pilot who are involved in decisions that are required to operate a flight safely.

2. Exhibits instructional knowledge of common errors related to crew resource management by describing—

    a. failure to place and secure essential materials and equipment for easy access during flight.
    b. improper adjustment of equipment and controls.
    c. failure to brief occupants on emergency procedures, rotor blade avoidance, and use of safety belts and shoulder harnesses.
    d. failure to utilize all available human resources, maintenance personnel, weather briefers, air traffic control, and other groups routinely working with the pilot who are involved in decisions that are required to operate a flight safely.

3. Demonstrates and simultaneously explains crew resource management from an instructional standpoint.

C. TASK: ENGINE STARTING AND ROTOR ENGAGEMENT

REFERENCES: FAA-H-8083-9, FAA-H-8083-21, AC 91-13, AC 91-42; FAA-S-8081-15, FAA-S-8081-16; Rotorcraft Flight Manual.

Objective. To determine that the applicant:

1. Exhibits instructional knowledge of the elements of engine starting and rotor engagement, as appropriate to the helicopter used for the practical test, by describing—

   a. safety precautions related to engine starting and rotor engagement.
   b. proper positioning of helicopter to avoid hazards.
   c. use of external power.
   d. effect of atmospheric conditions on engine starting and rotor engagement.
   e. importance of proper friction adjustment.
   f. importance of following the appropriate checklist.
   g. adjustment of engine and flight controls during engine start and rotor engagement.
   h. prevention of undesirable helicopter movement during and after engine start and rotor engagement.

2. Exhibits instructional knowledge of common errors related to engine starting and rotor engagement by describing—

   a. failure to use or improper use of checklist.
   b. exceeding starter time limitations.
   c. excessive engine RPM and/or temperatures during start.
   d. failure to ensure adequate main rotor or tail rotor clearance.

3. Demonstrates and simultaneously explains engine starting and rotor engagement from an instructional standpoint.

D. TASK: BEFORE TAKEOFF CHECK

REFERENCES: FAA-H-8083-9, FAA-H-8083-21; FAA-S-8081-15, FAA-S-8081-16; Rotorcraft Flight Manual.

Objective. To determine that the applicant:

1. Exhibits instructional knowledge of the elements of the before takeoff check by describing—

   a. division of attention inside and outside the cockpit.
   b. importance of following the checklist and responding to each item.
   c. reasons for ensuring suitable engine temperatures and pressures for run-up and takeoff.
   d. method used to determine that the helicopter is in safe operating condition.
   e. importance of reviewing emergency procedures.
   f. method used for ensuring that takeoff area or path is free of hazards.
   g. method used for ensuring adequate clearance from other traffic.

2. Exhibits instructional knowledge of common errors related to the before takeoff check by describing—

   a. failure to use or the improper use of the checklist.
   b. acceptance of marginal helicopter performance.
   c. an improper check of controls.

3. Demonstrates and simultaneously explains a before takeoff check from an instructional standpoint.
4. Analyzes and corrects simulated common errors related to a before takeoff check.

VI. AREA OF OPERATION: AIRPORT AND HELIPORT OPERATIONS

NOTE: The examiner shall select at least one TASK.

A. TASK: RADIO COMMUNICATIONS AND ATC LIGHT SIGNALS

REFERENCES: AIM; FAA-S-8081-15, FAA-S-8081-16; 14 CFR part 91.

Objective. To determine that the applicant:

1. Exhibits instructional knowledge of the elements of radio communications and ATC light signals by describing—

   a. selection and use of appropriate radio frequencies.
   b. recommended procedure and phraseology for radio voice communications.
   c. receipt, acknowledgment of, and compliance with, ATC clearances and other instructions.
   d. prescribed procedure for radio communications failure.
   e. interpretation of, and compliance with, ATC light signals.

2. Exhibits instructional knowledge of common errors related to radio communications and ATC light signals by describing—

   a. use of improper frequencies.
   b. improper techniques and phraseologies when using radio voice communications.
   c. failure to acknowledge, or properly comply with, ATC clearances and other instructions.
   d. use of improper procedures for radio communications failure.
   e. failure to understand, or to properly comply with, ATC light signals.

B. TASK: TRAFFIC PATTERNS

REFERENCES: FAA-H-8083-9, FAA-H-8083-21; 14 CFR part 91; AIM; FAA-S-8081-15, FAA-S-8081-16, AC 90-42, AC 90-48, AC 90-66

Objective. To determine that the applicant:

1. Exhibits instructional knowledge of the elements of traffic pattern operations by describing—

   a. operations at controlled and uncontrolled airports and heliports.
   b. adherence to traffic pattern procedures, instructions, and appropriate regulations.
   c. how to maintain appropriate spacing from other traffic.
   d. how to maintain desired ground track.
   e. wind shear and wake turbulence.
   f. orientation with landing area or heliport in use.
   g. how to establish an approach to the landing area or heliport.
   h. use of checklist.

2. Exhibits instructional knowledge of common errors related to traffic patterns by describing—

   a. failure to comply with traffic pattern instructions, procedures, and rules.
   b. improper correction for wind drift.
   c. inadequate spacing from other traffic.
   d. improper altitude or airspeed control.

3. Demonstrates and simultaneously explains traffic patterns from an instructional standpoint.
4. Analyzes and corrects simulated common errors related to traffic patterns.

C. TASK: AIRPORT AND HELIPORT MARKINGS AND LIGHTING

REFERENCES: AIM; FAA-H-8083-25; FAA-S-8081-15, FAA-S-8081-16. AC 150/5340-1, AC 150/ 5340-18, AC-150/5340-30

Objective. To determine that the applicant exhibits instructional knowledge of the elements of airport and heliport markings and lighting by describing:

1. Identification and proper interpretation of airport and heliport markings.
2. Identification and proper interpretation of airport and heliport lighting.

VII. AREA OF OPERATION: HOVERING MANEUVERS

NOTE: The examiner shall select at least one TASK.

A. TASK: VERTICAL TAKEOFF AND LANDING

REFERENCES: FAA-H-8083-9, FAA-H-8083-21; FAA-S-8081-15, FAA-S-8081-16; Rotorcraft Flight Manual.

Objective. To determine that the applicant:

1. Exhibits instructional knowledge of the elements of a vertical takeoff and landing by describing—

   a. how to establish and maintain proper RPM.
   b. proper position of collective pitch, cyclic, and anti-torque pedals prior to initiating takeoff.
   c. ascending vertically, at a suitable rate, to the recommended hovering altitude, in headwind, crosswind, and tailwind conditions.
   d. descending vertically, at a suitable rate, to a selected touchdown point.
   e. touching down vertically in headwind, crosswind, and tailwind conditions.
   f. how to maintain desired heading during the maneuver.

2. Exhibits instructional knowledge of common errors related to a vertical takeoff and landing by describing—

   a. improper RPM control.
   b. failure to ascend and descend vertically at a suitable rate.
   c. failure to recognize and correct undesirable drift.
   d. improper heading control.
   e. terminating takeoff at an improper altitude.
   f. overcontrol of collective pitch, cyclic, or anti-torque pedals.
   g. failure to reduce collective pitch to the full-down position, smoothly and positively, upon surface contact.

3. Demonstrates and simultaneously explains a vertical takeoff and landing from an instructional standpoint.
4. Analyzes and corrects simulated common errors related to a vertical takeoff and landing.

B. TASK: SURFACE TAXI

NOTE: This TASK applies only to helicopters equipped with wheel-type landing gear.

REFERENCES: FAA-H-8083-9, FAA-H-8083-21; AIM; FAA-S-8081-15, FAA-S-8081-16; Rotorcraft Flight Manual.

Objective. To determine that the applicant:

1. Exhibits instructional knowledge of the elements of surface taxi by describing—

   a. positioning of cyclic and collective to begin forward movement.
   b. proper use of cyclic, collective, and brakes to control speed while taxiing.
   c. use of anti-torque pedals to maintain directional control.
   d. use of brakes during minimum radius turns.
   e. proper position of tailwheel (if applicable) locked or unlocked.
   f. positioning of controls to slow and stop helicopter.

2. Exhibits instructional knowledge of common errors related to surface taxi by describing—

   a. improper positioning of cyclic and collective to start and stop movement.
   b. improper use of brakes.
   c. hazards of taxiing too fast.
   d. improper use of anti-torque pedals.

3. Demonstrates and simultaneously explains surface taxi from an instructional standpoint.
4. Analyzes and corrects simulated common errors related to surface taxi.

C. TASK: HOVER TAXI

REFERENCES: FAA-H-8083-9, FAA-H-8083-21; AIM; FAA-S-8081-15, FAA-S-8081-16; Rotorcraft Flight Manual.

Objective. To determine that the applicant:

1. Exhibits instructional knowledge of the elements of hover taxi by describing—

   a. how to maintain proper Revolutions Per Minute (RPM).
   b. maintaining desired ground track and heading.
   c. how to make precise turns to headings.
   d. holding recommended hovering altitude.
   e. appropriate groundspeed.

2. Exhibits instructional knowledge of common errors related to hover taxi by describing—

   a. improper RPM control.
   b. improper control of heading and track.
   c. erratic altitude control.
   d. misuse of flight controls.

3. Demonstrates and simultaneously explains hover taxi from an instructional standpoint.
4. Analyzes and corrects simulated common errors related to hover taxi.

D. TASK: AIR TAXI

REFERENCES: FAA-H-8083-9, FAA-H-8083-21; AIM; FAA-S-8081-15, FAA-S-8081-16; Rotorcraft Flight Manual.

Objective. To determine that the applicant:

1. Exhibits instructional knowledge of the elements of air taxi by describing—

   a. how to maintain proper RPM.
   b. selection of an altitude and airspeed appropriate for the operation.
   c. proper use of collective pitch, cyclic, and anti-torque pedals to maintain desired track and groundspeed in headwind and crosswind conditions.
   d. compensation for wind effect.

2. Exhibits instructional knowledge of common errors related to air taxi by describing—

   a. improper RPM control.
   b. erratic altitude and airspeed control.
   c. improper use of collective pitch, cyclic, and anti-torque pedals during operation.
   d. improper use of controls to compensate for wind effect.

3. Demonstrates and simultaneously explains air taxi from an instructional standpoint.
4. Analyzes and corrects simulated common errors related to air taxi.

E. TASK: SLOPE OPERATION

REFERENCES: FAA-H-8083-9, FAA-H-8083-21; FAA-S-8081-16; Rotorcraft Flight Manual.

Objective. To determine that the applicant:

1. Exhibits instructional knowledge of the elements of a slope operation by describing—

    a. factors to consider in selection of slope.
    b. planning and performance of a slope operation, considering wind effect, obstacles, and discharging of passengers.
    c. effect of slope surface texture.
    d. how to maintain proper RPM.
    e. control technique during descent to touchdown on a slope.
    f. use of brakes (if applicable).
    g. factors that should be considered to avoid dynamic rollover.
    h. technique during a slope takeoff and departure.

2. Exhibits instructional knowledge of common errors related to a slope operation by describing—

    a. improper planning selection of, approach to, or departure from the slope.
    b. failure to consider wind effects.
    c. improper RPM control.
    d. turning tail of the helicopter upslope.
    e. lowering downslope skid or wheels too rapidly.
    f. sliding downslope.
    g. improper use of brakes (if applicable).
    h. conditions that, if allowed to develop, may result in dynamic rollover.

3. Demonstrates and simultaneously explains a slope operation from an instructional standpoint.
4. Analyzes and corrects simulated common errors related to a slope operation.

VIII. AREA OF OPERATION: TAKEOFFS, LANDINGS, AND GO-AROUNDS

NOTE: The examiner shall select at least one takeoff TASK and one approach TASK.

A. TASK: NORMAL AND CROSSWIND TAKEOFF AND CLIMB

REFERENCES: FAA-H-8083-9, FAA-H-8083-21; FAA-S-8081-15, FAA-S-8081-16; Rotorcraft Flight Manual.

Objective. To determine that the applicant:

1. Exhibits instructional knowledge of the elements of a normal and crosswind takeoff and climb by describing—

   a. consideration of wind conditions.
   b. factors affecting takeoff and climb performance.
   c. how to maintain proper RPM.
   d. how to establish a stationary position on the surface or a stabilized hover, prior to takeoff in headwind and crosswind conditions.
   e. presence of effective translational lift.
   f. acceleration to a normal climb.
   g. climb airspeed and power setting.
   h. crosswind correction and ground track during climb.

2. Exhibits instructional knowledge of common errors related to a normal and crosswind takeoff and climb by describing—

   a. improper RPM control.
   b. improper use of cyclic, collective pitch, or anti-torque pedals.
   c. failure to use sufficient power to avoid settling prior to entering effective translational lift.
   d. improper coordination of attitude and power during initial phase of climb-out.
   e. failure to establish and maintain climb power and airspeed.
   f. drift during climb.

3. Demonstrates and simultaneously explains a normal or a crosswind takeoff and climb from an instructional standpoint.
4. Analyzes and corrects simulated common errors related to a normal or a crosswind takeoff and climb.

B. TASK: MAXIMUM PERFORMANCE TAKEOFF AND CLIMB

REFERENCES: FAA-H-8083-9, FAA-H-8083-21; FAA-S-8081-15, FAA-S-8081-16; Rotorcraft Flight Manual.

Objective. To determine that the applicant:

1. Exhibits instructional knowledge of the elements of a maximum performance takeoff and climb by describing—

    a. importance of considering performance data, to include height/velocity diagram.
    b. factors related to takeoff and climb performance of the aircraft.
    c. how to establish and maintain proper RPM.
    d. preparatory technique prior to increasing collective pitch to initiate takeoff.
    e. technique to initiate takeoff and establish a forward climb attitude to clear obstacles
    f. transition to normal climb power and airspeed.
    g. crosswind correction and track during climb.

2. Exhibits instructional knowledge of common errors related to a maximum performance takeoff and climb by describing—

    a. failure to consider performance data, including height/velocity diagram.
    b. improper RPM control.
    c. improper use of cyclic, collective pitch, or anti-torque pedals.
    d. failure to use the predetermined power setting for establishing attitude and airspeed appropriate to the obstacles to be cleared.
    e. failure to resume normal climb power and airspeed after obstacle clearance.
    f. drift during climb.

3. Demonstrates and simultaneously explains a maximum performance takeoff and climb from an instructional standpoint.
4. Analyzes and corrects simulated common errors related to a maximum performance takeoff and climb.

C. TASK: ROLLING TAKEOFF

NOTE: This TASK applies only to helicopters equipped with wheel-type landing gear.

REFERENCES: FAA-H-8083-9, FAA-H-8083-21; FAA-S-8081-15, FAA-S-8081-16; Rotorcraft Flight Manual.

Objective. To determine that the applicant:

1. Exhibits instructional knowledge of the elements of a rolling takeoff by describing—

   a. situations where this maneuver is recommended.
   b. factors related to takeoff and climb performance of the aircraft.
   c. how to establish and maintain proper RPM.
   d. preparatory technique prior to initiating takeoff.
   e. how to initiate forward accelerating movement on the surface.
   f. indication of reaching effective translational lift.
   g. transition to a normal climb airspeed and power setting.
   h. crosswind correction and track during climb.

2. Exhibits instructional knowledge of common errors related to a rolling takeoff by describing—

   a. improper RPM control.
   b. improper use of cyclic, collective pitch, or anti-torque pedals.
   c. failure to maintain heading and ground track.
   d. failure to attain effective translational lift prior to attempting transition to flight.
   e. use of excessive forward cyclic during the surface run.
   f. settling back to the takeoff surface after becoming airborne.
   g. excessive altitude prior to attaining climb airspeed.
   h. failure to establish and maintain climb power and airspeed.

3. Demonstrates and simultaneously explains a rolling takeoff from an instructional standpoint.
4. Analyzes and corrects simulated common errors related to a rolling takeoff.

D. TASK: NORMAL AND CROSSWIND APPROACH

REFERENCES: FAA-H-8083-9, FAA-H-8083-21; FAA-S-8081-15, FAA-S-8081-16; Rotorcraft Flight Manual.

Objective. To determine that the applicant:

1. Exhibits instructional knowledge of the elements of a normal and crosswind approach by describing—

   a. factors affecting performance.
   b. how to maintain proper RPM.
   c. establishment and maintenance of the recommended approach angle and rate of closure.
   d. coordination of flight controls.
   e. crosswind correction and ground track.
   f. loss of effective translational lift.
   g. how to terminate the approach.

2. Exhibits instructional knowledge of common errors related to a normal and crosswind approach by describing—

   a. improper RPM control.
   b. improper approach angle.
   c. improper use of cyclic to control rate of closure and collective pitch to control approach angle.
   d. failure to coordinate pedal corrections with power changes.
   e. failure to arrive at the termination point at zero groundspeed.

3. Demonstrates and simultaneously explains a normal or a crosswind approach from an instructional standpoint.
4. Analyzes and corrects simulated common errors related to a normal or a crosswind approach.

E. TASK: STEEP APPROACH

REFERENCES: FAA-H-8083-9, FAA-H-8083-21; FAA-S-8081-15, FAA-S-8081-16; Rotorcraft Flight Manual.

Objective. To determine that the applicant:

1. Exhibits instructional knowledge of the elements of a steep approach by describing—

   a. purpose of the maneuver.
   b. importance of considering performance data, to include height/velocity diagram.
   c. selection of proper approach angle for obstacle clearance.
   d. how to maintain proper RPM.
   e. establishment and maintenance of the appropriate approach angle and rate of closure.
   f. coordination of flight controls.
   g. crosswind correction and ground track.
   h. location where effective translational lift is lost. .
   i. how to terminate the approach.

2. Exhibits instructional knowledge of common errors related to a steep approach by describing—

   a. improper approach angle.
   b. improper RPM control.
   c. improper use of cyclic to control rate of closure and collective pitch to control approach angle.
   d. failure to coordinate pedal corrections with power changes.
   e. failure to arrive at the termination point at zero groundspeed.
   f. inability to determine location where effective translational lift is lost.

3. Demonstrates and simultaneously explains a steep approach from an instructional standpoint.
4. Analyzes and corrects simulated common errors related to a steep approach.

F. TASK: SHALLOW APPROACH AND RUNNING/ROLL-ON LANDING

REFERENCES: FAA-H-8083-9, FAA-H-8083-21; FAA-S-8081-15, FAA-S-8081-16; Rotorcraft Flight Manual.

Objective. To determine that the applicant:

1. Exhibits instructional knowledge of the elements of a shallow approach and running/roll-on landing by describing—

   a. purpose of the maneuver.
   b. effect of landing surface texture.
   c. factors affecting performance.
   d. how to maintain proper RPM.
   e. obstacles and other hazards, which should be considered.
   f. establishment and maintenance of the recommended approach angle and rate of closure.
   g. coordination of flight controls.
   h. crosswind correction and ground track.
   i. loss of effective translational lift.
   j. transition from descent to surface contact.
   k. flight control technique after surface contact.

2. Exhibits instructional knowledge of common errors related to a shallow approach and running/roll-on landing by describing—

   a. improper RPM control.
   b. improper approach angle.
   c. improper use of cyclic to control rate of closure and collective pitch to control approach angle.
   d. failure to coordinate pedal corrections with power changes.
   e. failure to maintain a speed that will take advantage of effective translational lift during the final phase of approach.
   f. touching down at an excessive groundspeed.
   g. failure to touch down in appropriate attitude.
   h. failure to maintain directional control after touchdown.

3. Demonstrates and simultaneously explains a shallow approach and running/roll-on landing from an instructional standpoint.
4. Analyzes and corrects simulated common errors related to a shallow approach and running/roll-on landing.

G. TASK: GO-AROUND

REFERENCES: FAA-H-8083-9, FAA-H-8083-21; FAA-S-8081-15, FAA-S-8081-16; Rotorcraft Flight Manual.

Objective. To determine that the applicant:

1. Exhibits instructional knowledge of the elements of a go-around by describing—

   a. situations where a go-around is necessary.
   b. importance of making a timely decision, considering obstacles, loss of translational lift, and engine response time.
   c. proper use of power throughout maneuver.
   d. timely and coordinated application of flight controls during transition to climb attitude.
   e. proper track and obstacle clearance during climb.

2. Exhibits instructional knowledge of common errors related to a go-around by describing—

   a. failure to recognize a situation where a go-around is necessary.
   b. hazards of delaying the decision to go around.
   c. improper application of flight controls during transition to climb attitude.
   d. failure to control drift and clear obstacles safely.

3. Demonstrates and simultaneously explains a go-around from an instructional standpoint.
4. Analyzes and corrects simulated common errors related to a go-around.

H. TASK: APPROACH AND LANDING WITH SIMULATED POWERPLANT FAILURE - MULTIENGINE HELICOPER

NOTE: In a multiengine helicopter maneuvering to a landing, the applicant should follow a procedure that simulates the loss of one powerplant.

REFERENCE(S): FAA-H-8083-21; Rotorcraft Flight Manual

Objective. To determine that the applicant:

1. Exhibits instructional knowledge of the elements an approach and landing with simulated powerplant failure.
2. Exhibits adequate knowledge of maneuvering to a landing with a powerplant inoperative, including the controllability factors associated with maneuvering, and the applicable emergency procedures.

3. Selects a suitable touchdown point.
4. Maintains, prior to beginning the final approach segment, the desired altitude ± 100 feet, the desired airspeed ± 10 knots, the desired heading ± 5°, and maintains desired track.
5. Establishes the approach and landing configuration appropriate for the runway or landing area, and adjusts the powerplant controls as required.
6. Maintains a normal approach angle and recommended airspeed to the point of transition to touchdown.
7. Terminates the approach in a smooth transition to touchdown.
8. Completes the after-landing checklist items in a timely manner, after clearing the landing area, and as recommended by the manufacturer.
9. Exhibits instructional knowledge of common errors related to approach and landing with simulated powerplant failure by describing—

   a. hazards resulting from not following manufacturer's recommended procedures in the event of a powerplant failure.
   b. failure of the pilot to follow the appropriate checklist.

10. Demonstrates and simultaneously explains approaching and landing procedures with a simulated powerplant failure.
11. Analyzes and corrects simulated common errors related to an approach and landing with simulated powerplant failure.

IX. AREA OF OPERATION: FUNDAMENTALS OF FLIGHT

NOTE: The examiner shall select at least one TASK.

A. TASK: STRAIGHT-AND-LEVEL FLIGHT

REFERENCES: FAA-H-8083-9, FAA-H-8083-21.

Objective. To determine that the applicant:

1. Exhibits instructional knowledge of the elements of straight-and-level flight by describing—

   a. effect and use of flight controls.
   b. the Integrated Flight Instruction method.
   c. trim technique.
   d. methods that can be used to overcome tenseness and over controlling.

2. Exhibits instructional knowledge of common errors related to straight-and-level flight by describing—

   a. improper coordination of flight controls.
   b. failure to cross-check and correctly interpret outside and instrument references.
   c. faulty trim technique.

3. Demonstrates and simultaneously explains straight-and-level flight from an instructional standpoint.
4. Analyzes and corrects simulated common errors related to straight-and-level flight.

B. TASK: LEVEL TURNS

REFERENCES: FAA-H-8083-9, FAA-H-8083-21.

Objective. To determine that the applicant:

1. Exhibits instructional knowledge of the elements of level turns by describing—

   a. effect and use of flight controls.
   b. the Integrated Flight Instruction method.
   c. trim technique.
   d. methods that can be used to overcome tenseness and over controlling.

2. Exhibits instructional knowledge of common errors related to level turns by describing—

   a. improper coordination of flight controls.
   b. failure to cross-check and correctly interpret outside and instrument references.
   c. faulty trim technique.

3. Demonstrates and simultaneously explains level turns from an instructional standpoint.
4. Analyzes and corrects simulated common errors related to level turns.

C. TASK: STRAIGHT CLIMBS AND CLIMBING TURNS

REFERENCES: FAA-H-8083-9, FAA-H-8083-21.

Objective. To determine that the applicant:

1. Exhibits instructional knowledge of the elements of straight climbs and climbing turns by describing—

   a. effect and use of flight controls.
   b. the Integrated Flight Instruction method.
   c. trim technique.
   d. methods that can be used to overcome tenseness and over controlling.

2. Exhibits instructional knowledge of common errors related to straight climbs and climbing turns by describing—

   a. improper coordination of flight controls.
   b. failure to cross-check and correctly interpret outside and instrument references.
   c. faulty trim technique.

3. Demonstrates and simultaneously explains straight climbs and climbing turns from an instructional standpoint.
4. Analyzes and corrects simulated common errors related to straight climbs and climbing turns.

D. TASK: STRAIGHT DESCENTS AND DESCENDING TURNS

REFERENCES: FAA-H-8083-9, FAA-H-8083-21.

Objective. To determine that the applicant:

1. Exhibits instructional knowledge of the elements of straight descents and descending turns by describing—

   a. effect and use of flight controls.
   b. the Integrated Flight Instruction method.
   c. trim technique.
   d. methods that can be used to overcome tenseness and over controlling.

2. Exhibits instructional knowledge of common errors related to straight descents and descending turns by describing—

   a. improper coordination of flight controls.
   b. failure to cross-check and correctly interpret outside and instrument references.
   c. faulty trim technique.

3. Demonstrates and simultaneously explains straight descents and descending turns from an instructional standpoint.
4. Analyzes and corrects simulated common errors related to straight descents and descending turns.

X. AREA OF OPERATION: PERFORMANCE MANEUVERS

NOTE: The examiner shall select at least TASK B or C. In addition, applicant shall provide a helicopter appropriate for demonstrating touchdown autorotations.

A. TASK: RAPID DECELERATION

REFERENCES: FAA-H-8083-9, FAA-H-8083-21; FAA-S-8081-15, FAA-S-8081-16; Rotorcraft Flight Manual.

Objective. To determine that the applicant:

1. Exhibits instructional knowledge of the elements of a rapid deceleration by describing—

   a. purpose of the maneuver.
   b. how to maintain proper RPM throughout maneuver.
   c. evaluation of wind direction and speed, terrain, and obstructions.
   d. proper use of anti-torque pedals.
   e. selection of an altitude that will permit safe clearance between tail boom and terrain.
   f. coordinated use of cyclic and collective controls throughout maneuver.

2. Exhibits instructional knowledge of common errors related to a rapid deceleration by describing—

   a. improper RPM control.
   b. improper use of anti-torque pedals.
   c. improper coordination of cyclic and collective controls.
   d. failure to properly control the rate of deceleration.
   e. stopping of forward motion in a tail-low attitude.
   f. failure to maintain safe clearance over terrain.

3. Demonstrates and simultaneously explains a rapid deceleration from an instructional standpoint.
4. Analyzes and corrects simulated common errors related to a rapid deceleration.

B. TASK: STRAIGHT-IN AUTOROTATION

REFERENCES: FAA-H-8083-9, FAA-H-8083-21; FAA-S-8081-15; Rotorcraft Flight Manual.

Objective. To determine that the applicant:

1. Exhibits instructional knowledge of the elements of a straight-in autorotation by describing—

   a. purpose of maneuver.
   b. selection of a suitable touchdown area.
   c. how to maintain proper engine and rotor RPM.
   d. evaluation of wind direction and speed.
   e. effect of density altitude, gross weight, rotor RPM, airspeed, and wind to determine a touchdown point.
   f. how and at what point maneuver is initiated.
   g. flight control coordination, aircraft attitude, and autorotational speed.
   h. deceleration, collective pitch application, and touchdown technique, or
   i. technique for performing a power recovery to a hover.

2. Exhibits instructional knowledge of common errors related to a straight-in autorotation by describing—

   a. improper engine and rotor RPM control.
   b. uncoordinated use of flight controls, particularly anti-torque pedals.
   c. improper attitude and airspeed during descent.
   d. improper judgment and technique during termination.

3. Demonstrates and simultaneously explains a straight-in autorotation to touchdown from an instructional standpoint.
4. Analyzes and corrects simulated common errors related to a straight-in autorotation.

C. TASK: 180° AUTOROTATION

REFERENCES: FAA-H-8083-9, FAA-H-8083-21; FAA-S-8081-16; Rotorcraft Flight Manual.

Objective. To determine that the applicant:

1. Exhibits instructional knowledge of the elements of a 180° autorotation by describing—

   a. purpose of maneuver.
   b. selection of a suitable touchdown area.
   c. how to maintain proper engine and rotor RPM.
   d. evaluation of wind direction and speed.
   e. effect of density altitude, gross weight, rotor RPM, airspeed, and wind to determine a touchdown point.
   f. how and at what point the maneuver is initiated.
   g. flight control coordination, aircraft attitude, and autorotation airspeed.
   h. proper planning and performance of the autorotative turn.
   i. deceleration, collective pitch application, and touchdown technique, or
   j. technique for performing a power recovery to a hover.

2. Exhibits instructional knowledge of common errors related to a 180° autorotation by describing—

   a. improper engine and rotor RPM control.
   b. uncoordinated use of flight controls, particularly anti-torque pedals.
   c. improper attitude and airspeed during descent.
   d. improper judgment and technique during the termination.

3. Demonstrates and simultaneously explains a 180° autorotation to touchdown from an instructional standpoint.
4. Analyzes and corrects simulated common errors related to a 180° autorotation.

XI. AREA OF OPERATION: EMERGENCY OPERATIONS

NOTE: The examiner shall select at least one TASK from A, B, C, or D to be accomplished in flight and at least one TASK from E, F, G, H, I, or J to be accomplished orally on the ground.

A. TASK: POWER FAILURE AT A HOVER

REFERENCES: FAA-H-8083-9, FAA-H-8083-21; FAA-S-8081-15, FAA-S-8081-16; Rotorcraft Flight Manual.

Objective. To determine that the applicant:

1. Exhibits instructional knowledge of the elements related to power failure at a hover by describing—

   a. recognition of power failure.
   b. how to maintain a constant heading.
   c. correction for drift.
   d. effect of density altitude, height above the surface, gross weight, wind, and rotor RPM on performance.
   e. autorotation and touchdown technique from a stationary or forward hover.

2. Exhibits instructional knowledge of common errors related to power failure at a hover by describing—

   a. failure to apply correct and adequate pedal when power is reduced.
   b. failure to correct drift prior to touchdown.
   c. improper application of collective pitch.
   d. failure to touch down in a level attitude.

3. Demonstrates and simultaneously explains a simulated power failure at a hover from an instructional standpoint.
4. Analyzes and corrects simulated common errors related to a simulated power failure at a hover.

B. TASK: POWER FAILURE AT ALTITUDE

REFERENCES: FAA-H-8083-9, FAA-H-8083-21; FAA-S-8081-15, FAA-S-8081-16; Rotorcraft Flight Manual.

NOTE: Examiner shall direct the applicant to terminate this TASK with a power recovery at an altitude high enough to ensure a safe touchdown could be accomplished in the event of an actual power failure.

Objective. To determine that the applicant:

1. Exhibits instructional knowledge of the elements related to power failure at altitude by describing—

    a. importance of being continuously aware of suitable landing areas.
    b. technique for establishing and maintaining proper rotor RPM, airspeed, and pedal trim during autorotation.
    c. method used to evaluate wind direction and speed.
    d. effect of density altitude, gross weight, rotor RPM, airspeed, and wind to determine landing area.
    e. selection of a suitable landing area.
    f. planning and performance of approach to the selected landing area.
    g. importance of dividing attention between flying the approach and accomplishing the emergency procedure, as time permits.
    h. techniques that can be used to compensate for undershooting or overshooting selected landing area.
    i. when and how to terminate approach.

2. Exhibits instructional knowledge of common errors related to power failure at altitude by describing—

    a. failure to promptly recognize the emergency, establish and maintain proper rotor RPM, and confirm engine condition.
    b. improper judgment in selection of a landing area.
    c. failure to estimate approximate wind direction and speed.
    d. uncoordinated use of flight controls during autorotation entry and descent.
    e. improper attitude and airspeed during autorotation entry and descent.
    f. failure to fly the most suitable pattern for existing situation.
    g. failure to accomplish the emergency procedure, as time permits.
    h. **undershooting** or overshooting selected landing area.
    i. **uncoordin**ated use of flight controls during power recovery.

3. Demonstrates and simultaneously explains a simulated power failure at altitude from an instructional standpoint.
4. Analyzes and corrects simulated common errors related to power failure at altitude.

C. TASK: SETTLING-WITH-POWER

REFERENCES: FAA-H-8083-9, FAA-H-8083-21; FAA-S-8081-15, FAA-S-8081-16; Rotorcraft Flight Manual.

Objective. To determine that the applicant:

1. Exhibits instructional knowledge of the elements related to settling-with-power by describing—

   a. conditions that are likely to result in settling-with-power.
   b. timely recognition of settling-with-power.
   c. techniques for recovery.

2. Exhibits instructional knowledge of common errors related to settling-with-power by describing—

   a. failure to recognize conditions that are conducive to development of settling-with-power.
   b. failure to detect first indications of settling-with-power.
   c. improper use of controls during recovery.

3. Demonstrates and simultaneously explains settling-with-power from an instructional standpoint.

D. TASK: LOW ROTOR RPM RECOVERY

NOTE: The examiner may accomplish this TASK orally if the helicopter used for the practical test has a governor that cannot be disabled.

REFERENCES: FAA-H-8083-9, FAA-H-8083-21; FAA-S-8081-15, FAA-S-8081-16; Rotorcraft Flight Manual.

Objective. To determine that the applicant:

1. Exhibits instructional knowledge of the elements related to low rotor RPM recovery by describing—

   a. conditions that are likely to result in low rotor RPM.
   b. potential problems from low rotor RPM if not corrected timely.
   c. techniques for recovery.

2. Exhibits instructional knowledge of common errors related to low rotor RPM recovery by describing—

   a. failure to recognize conditions that are conducive to the development of low rotor RPM.
   b. failure to detect the development of low rotor RPM and to initiate prompt corrective action.
   c. improper use of controls.

3. Demonstrates and simultaneously explains low rotor RPM recovery from an instructional standpoint.

E. TASK: ANTI-TORQUE SYSTEM FAILURE

REFERENCES: FAA-H-8083-9, FAA-H-8083-21; FAA-S-8081-15, FAA-S-8081-16; Helicopter Flight Manual.

Objective. To determine that the applicant exhibits instructional knowledge of the elements related to anti-torque system failure by describing:

1. Helicopter aerodynamics related to failure.
2. Indications of failure.
3. Recommended pilot technique to maintain controlled flight.
4. How to select a landing area.
5. Recommended technique to accomplish a safe landing, when failure occurs.

F. TASK: DYNAMIC ROLLOVER

REFERENCES: FAA-H-8083-21; AC 90-87; FAA-S-8081-15, FAA-S-8081-16; Rotorcraft Flight Manual.

Objective. To determine that the applicant exhibits instructional knowledge of the elements related to dynamic rollover by describing:

1. Helicopter aerodynamics involved.
2. How interaction between anti-torque thrust, crosswind, slope, cyclic and collective pitch control contribute to dynamic rollover.
3. Preventive actions used for takeoffs and landings on different surfaces.

G. TASK: GROUND RESONANCE

REFERENCES: FAA-H-8083-21; FAA-S-8081-15, FAA-S-8081-16; Rotorcraft Flight Manual.

Objective. To determine that the applicant exhibits instructional knowledge of the elements related to ground resonance by describing:

1. Aerodynamics involved and association with a fully articulated rotor system.
2. Conditions that are conducive to the development of ground resonance.
3. Preventive actions used for takeoffs and landings on different surfaces.

H. TASK: LOW "G" CONDITIONS

REFERENCE: Rotorcraft Flight Manual.

Objective. To determine that the applicant exhibits instructional knowledge of the elements of low "G" conditions by describing:

1. Situations that will cause a low "G" condition.
2. Recognition of low "G" conditions.
3. Proper recovery procedures to prevent mast bumping.
4. Effects of this condition on different types of rotor systems.

I. TASK: SYSTEMS AND EQUIPMENT MALFUNCTIONS

REFERENCES: FAA-H-8083-21; FAA-S-8081-15, FAA-S-8081-16; Rotorcraft Flight Manual.

Objective. To determine that the applicant exhibits instructional knowledge of the elements related to systems and equipment malfunctions by describing recommended pilot action, appropriate to the helicopter used for the practical test, in the following areas:

1. Smoke or fire during ground or flight operations.
2. Engine/oil and fuel system.
3. Carburetor or induction icing.
4. Hydraulic system.
5. Electrical system.
6. Flight controls.
7. Rotor/drive system.
8. Pitot/static system.
9. Any other system or equipment.

J. TASK: EMERGENCY EQUIPMENT AND SURVIVAL GEAR

REFERENCES: FAA-H-8083-21; Rotorcraft Flight Manual.

Objective. To determine that the applicant exhibits instructional knowledge of the elements related to emergency equipment and survival gear appropriate to the helicopter used for the practical test by describing:

1. Location in the helicopter.
2. Method of operation or use.
3. Servicing.
4. Storage.
5. Equipment and gear appropriate for operation in various climates, over various types of terrain, and over water.

XII. AREA OF OPERATION: SPECIAL OPERATIONS

NOTE: The examiner shall select at least one TASK.

A. TASK: CONFINED AREA OPERATION

REFERENCES: FAA-H-8083-9, FAA-H-8083-21; FAA-S-8081-16;
Rotorcraft Flight Manual.

Objective. To determine that the applicant:

1. Exhibits instructional knowledge of the elements of a confined area operation by describing—

    a. conduct of high and low reconnaissance.
    b. method used to evaluate wind direction and speed, turbulence, terrain, obstacles, and emergency landing areas.
    c. selection of a suitable approach path, termination point, and departure path.
    d. how to maintain proper RPM.
    e. how to track the selected approach path to the termination point, establishing an acceptable approach angle and rate of closure.
    f. factors that should be considered in determining whether to terminate at a hover or on the surface.
    g. conduct of ground reconnaissance and selection of a suitable takeoff point, considering wind and obstructions.
    h. factors affecting takeoff and climb performance.
    i. factors to consider in performing a takeoff and climb under various conditions.

2. Exhibits instructional knowledge of common errors related to a confined area operation by describing—

    a. failure to perform, or improper performance of high and low reconnaissance.
    b. failure to track the selected approach path or to fly an acceptable approach angle and rate of closure.
    c. improper RPM control.
    d. inadequate planning to ensure obstacle clearance during the approach or the departure.
    e. failure to consider emergency landing areas.
    f. failure to select a definite termination point during the high reconnaissance.
    g. failure to change the termination point, if conditions so dictate.
    h. failure to consider effect of wind direction or speed, turbulence, or loss of effective translational lift during the approach.

    i. improper takeoff and climb technique for existing conditions.

3. Demonstrates and simultaneously explains a confined area operation from an instructional standpoint.
4. Analyzes and corrects simulated common errors related to a confined area operation.

B. TASK: PINNACLE/PLATFORM OPERATION

REFERENCES: FAA-H-8083-9, FAA-H-8083-21; FAA-S-8081-16; Rotorcraft Flight Manual.

Objective. To determine that the applicant:

1. Exhibits instructional knowledge of the elements of a pinnacle/platform operation by describing—

   a. conduct of high and low reconnaissance.
   b. methods used to evaluate wind direction and speed, turbulence, terrain, obstacles, and emergency landing areas.
   c. selection of a suitable approach path, termination point, and departure path.
   d. how to maintain proper RPM.
   e. how to track the selected approach path to the termination point, and establish an acceptable approach angle and rate of closure.
   f. factors that should be considered in determining whether to terminate in a hover or on the surface.
   g. selection of a suitable takeoff point, considering wind and obstructions.
   h. factors affecting takeoff and climb performance.
   i. factors to consider in performing a takeoff and climb under various conditions.

2. Exhibits instructional knowledge of common errors related to a pinnacle/platform operation by describing—

   a. failure to perform, or improper performance of, high and low reconnaissance.
   b. failure to track selected approach path or to fly an acceptable approach angle and rate of closure.
   c. improper RPM control.
   d. inadequate planning to assure obstacle clearance during approach or departure.
   e. failure to consider emergency landing areas.
   f. failure to select a definite termination point during the high reconnaissance.
   g. failure to change the termination point, if conditions so dictate.
   h. failure to consider effect of wind direction or speed, turbulence, or loss of effective translational lift during the approach.
   i. improper takeoff and climb technique for existing conditions.

3. Demonstrates and simultaneously explains a pinnacle/platform operation from an instructional standpoint.
4. Analyzes and corrects simulated common errors related to a pinnacle/platform operation.

XIII. AREA OF OPERATION: POSTFLIGHT PROCEDURES

A. TASK: AFTER-LANDING AND SECURING

REFERENCES: FAA-H-8083-9; FAA-S-8081-15,
FAA-S-8081-16; Rotorcraft Flight Manual.

Objective. To determine that the applicant:

1. Exhibits instructional knowledge of the elements of after-landing and securing by describing—

   a. methods to minimize hazardous effects of rotor downwash during hovering to parking area.
   b. engine temperature stabilization and shutdown.
   c. method to secure rotor blades and cockpit.
   d. safety concerns for passenger(s) when exiting.
   e. postflight inspection to include use of checklist.
   f. refueling procedures, including safety concerns.

2. Exhibits instructional knowledge of common errors related to after-landing and securing by describing—

   a. hazards resulting from failure to follow recommended procedures.
   b. failure to conduct a postflight inspection and use a checklist.

3. Demonstrates and simultaneously explains after-landing and securing from an instructional standpoint.
4. Analyzes and corrects simulated common errors related to after-landing and securing.